THE NUCLEAR DILEMMA
a Christian Search
for Understanding

**A Report of the Committee of Inquiry
on the Nuclear Issue,
Commission on Peace, Episcopal Diocese of Washington**

May, 1987

*Come now, let us reason together,
saith the Lord . . .*

(Isaiah 1:18)

Forward Movement Publications
Cincinnati, Ohio

Distributed by arrangement with University Press of America.

©Committee of Inquiry on the Nuclear Issue, Commission on Peace, Episcopal Diocese of Washingtion.

Published by Forward Movement Publications, 412 Sycamore Street, Cincinnati, Ohio 45202. Printed in U.S.A.

ISBN 0 88028 071 9

Table of Contents

Foreword

The report of the Committee of Inquiry on the Nuclear Issue of the Diocese of Washington is subtitled "A Christian Search for Understanding." I welcome and commend the work of the committee and the initiative of the Bishop and Diocese of Washington in promoting it. They have creatively grasped the uniqueness of their locality in the nation's capital and have served us well in this undertaking. Especially I want to thank the committee for placing before us the task of the Christian search for understanding when dealing with the nuclear issue. It is easy to lose sight of this vital religious focus when one enters the world of international power politics and the "newspeak" of the nuclear age. So, let me state at the outset that the Epilogue, "A Policy Ethic," might well be the prologue to our continuing search.

The Nuclear Dilemma is a latchkey that I hope many will use to open their minds to the issues involved and to take active response to them. It stimulates us all to reason together. It truly has the potential "to infuse political decision making with the kind of statecraft...and the kind of compassion and redemptive love...so that Christian citizenship [could] indeed acquire a new meaning and become a channel of grace and renewal for the world," as the epilogue suggests.

Edmond Lee Browning
Presiding Bishop

When I asked Ambassador Vaky to make a study of the nuclear issues facing our world and a Chrisitan understanding of them, I was mindful of the special opportunity that we have in the Diocese of Washington. Because many of our church people are in positions of high responsibility in government we would be able to form a committee rich in experience. Further, that committee would be in a position to consult with those making the decisions that shape our world. A study by such a group could be useful not only to the Diocese of Washington but to the church as a whole, and perhaps even to our country at large.

As indicated in the preface, the initial draft of the study the committee made has been distributed throughout the United States and abroad as well. Comments have been received from a great many individuals of varied backgrounds and varied positions in life. With those comments the draft has been revised and events updated. This book is the result.

The book is not hortatory. The church makes many resolutions and we all, lay and cleric alike, preach the need for peace and goodwill, and resounding resolutions are good but not enough. The problem is how to make effective what we know and believe. How in this troubled, confused world do we move from the edge of the abyss to safer ground? What steps do we take to move to that high ground of human relations about which we preach and make resolutions?

When the Commission on Peace, of which the group who made this study is a committee, first met, the chairman asked each member to write a prayer that would express the purpose of the commission. Among the prayers was this one.

> Set me free, O God, from the bondage of my culture, my preconceptions, my patterns of thinking, and enable me, in the spirit of Him who makes all things

3

new, to work with all peoples for the control of the atom that it may be used not for destruction but for the glorious liberty of all people. This, I ask in the spirit of the One who came that all might have life and have it more abundantly, Jesus Christ, our Lord.

I commend this book to you because I believe it will be helpful to us to arrive at that high ground that we all seek. I also wish to express gratitude to Ambassador Vaky and the committee for the work that they have done and for the contribution they have made in helping us move to that safer, better, more peaceful world our Lord envisioned and we all desire so desperately.

The Right Reverend John T. Walker
Bishop of Washington

Preface

In February, 1982, the Rt. Rev. John T. Walker, Episcopal Bishop of Washington, appointed a Diocesan Commission on Peace in compliance with a request made by the 87th Convention of the Washington Diocese. The convention had requested that such a commission be named "to help the people of the Diocese fulfill the intention" of the October 1981 Pastoral Letter from the House of Bishops of the Episcopal Church, which had called upon church people to work for peace and for an end to the arms race.

In the course of its work, the Peace Commission found most of its attention drawn to the question of nuclear war and peace. The members of the commission recognized that the "nuclear issue" is extremely complex and multidimensional, involving different and interacting considerations beyond weapons themselves; that there are different interpretations of international realities and of national security and defense; and that, as a result, frustration, confusion and anxiety have become part of the public concern about nuclear weapons.

The Peace Commission, therefore, recommended to Bishop Walker that he designate a group of people to study the nuclear issue in depth, i.e., to sort out the different arguments and points of view, to consult experts and policy-makers, and, in particular, to examine both the moral/ethical and the political/security dimensions of these questions. It was felt that if a group undertook such a study, its findings might help church people think their way through the serious dilemmas posed by nuclear weapons.

In June 1983, therefore, Bishop Walker asked 16 persons—13 laity and 3 Episcopal clergy — to form a diocesan "Committee of Inquiry on the Nuclear Issue." (The list of members appears in the addenda). The committee began its work on June 21, 1983. Over the next two years it met with 45 experts and policymakers (listed in the addenda as witnesses), consulted a wide range of written works and published statements, and met almost weekly in intense and lengthy deliberations. In August

1985, the committee issued a draft report which was distributed to some 20 other dioceses, and to a large number of persons, experts and organizations outside of the Episcopal Church as well.

This — the committee's final report — represents a review and revision of that draft. In preparing it we took into account the many comments and criticisms of the draft which we received, and we sought to reflect both the changing realities of the nuclear issue and the evolving terms of the public debate.

Our inquiry parallels similar endeavors by others, notably the Pastoral Letter issued by the American Catholic Bishops in 1983, the two reports of the National Joint Committee on Peace of the Episcopal Church published in 1982 and 1985, and the Pastoral of the United Methodist Council of Bishops published in 1986. But it also differs from these in intent and purpose. This report is not an official document of the Episcopal Church. Nor is it a theological treatise; it is not meant to be either homiletic or exhortatory. It is simply a description of our inquiry — what we, as a group of ordinary church-going people, studied, how we reasoned, and what we concluded — all presented in the hope that it might be a vehicle to help others get a handle on the moral and political dilemmas involved in the nuclear issue.

We structured our inquiry as an examination of nuclear questions in the form in which they present themselves operationally in everyday life to our decision-makers and legislators, and to the average citizen, i.e., as secular political and security policy choices. Our report, therefore, focuses on the elements of public policy, because as a practical matter that is the arena in which decisions will be made and the prospects for peace or war determined. We sought to understand exactly what was at issue in the questions posed; to analyze the elements, arguments, options and rationales; and then to reason back inductively from the specific to the general — to the larger framework and principles which the specific problems reflected — looking at those from our perspective as American citizens and in terms of the relevant assumptions of our religious faith and its moral values.

We became convinced that, regardless of what has already been written and summarized, there is no substitute for people going through this kind of analyzing process for themselves, even if that traverses already plowed ground. If some of this report has the flavor of a college textbook, then, that is somewhat deliberate and unavoidable.

While we began our deliberations by defining topography, as it were, we soon felt compelled to go beyond the mere description of various options and issues to reach conclusions about these matters ourselves — to decide where *we* stand. Indeed, we felt that an account of how and why we ended up where we did would be substantially more helpful to persons struggling through these tasks than a simple cataloging of alternative arguments.

We have been conscious that, in the process, we are in effect taking part in what may be described as a major, on-going, national public debate. Our report *does* present an argument. But it does so in the spirit of describing rather than prescribing, of laying out *our* conclusions. Some readers may not agree with our arguments, but we hope that all will find themselves stimulated and challenged to think through these issues themselves. For in the final analysis our objective has been less to produce a consensus than to raise consciousness about these issues and to stimulate further contemplation and study of them.

Our readers will also note that we did not attempt to analyze every specific operational problem currently at issue. We found it more useful instead to probe the underlying premises, assumptions and beliefs — the mind-sets — which give shape to policy and which are reflected in strategies and operational decisions. We ascribe considerable importance to this matter of mind-sets, for they determine what we "see" and what we "do." Nor does our report attempt a detailed set of blueprints for the future. Rather we concentrated on what we have labeled "controlling visions," by which we mean the aims, moral values and reference points which should guide the political and prudential — i.e., secular — decisions that now confront the nation. We tried, in short, to understand the world as it exists, not only in the sense of structures and conditions *on* which we need to work, but also *with* which we must work — and we believe the nuance is important.

We are aware that our report does not adequately treat other important nuclear weapons-related issues, such as the spread of nuclear weapons to other countries or the possibility of terrorists acquiring them. Nor does it deal with the whole question of conventional arms and conventional war. This is not because these matters are not important, but because finite limits of space and time required us to restrict our choices. We decided to focus on the U.S.-Soviet relationship because of our conviction that the most serious and catastrophic threat to the world now and for the foreseeable future comes from the possibility of nuclear exchanges between the superpowers.

When we began our inquiry together, we were as ordinary church people: fallible and prayerful — mindful of what we had learned throughout our lives of Christian doctrine, ethics, and biblical witness. As we reasoned and deliberated together, we did not come to our political conclusions and then stop to ask ourselves if they conformed to our religious traditions. Our faith was an integral part of ourselves, and the sense of prudence, justice and mercy which each of us brought to the task conditioned all of our thinking.

Our readers will not find frequent religious references in this report of our pilgrimage. Rather we have concentrated most of the discussion of religious, ethical and moral dimensions in one chapter (Chapter VI). We did so, not because we conceive of them as separate or separable from temporal political matters, but for editorial and analytical purposes, i.e., as a way to provide more conscious attention to and examination of these dimensions.

No doubt this report is less hortatory and theological than some readers may have expected or preferred. But, to repeat an earlier point, our focus on "policy" was deliberate. We struggled as a group with the "real life" condition each of us faces as Christians and citizens: how to respond in this temporal world to secular issues which fall squarely in the middle of the tension to which each Christian is subject between the requirements of the temporal world and the imperatives of our religious faith. How do we deal in these instances with consequences and intentions, with "what is right" and "what is good?" As secular as this report may seem to some, therefore, we earnestly believe that it can be fairly described as a "Christian search for understanding," for grappling with the tensions into which we are thrust every day of our lives.

Finally, we emphasize that the report is a group document. As such it represents the broad consensus of all members of the Committee of Inquiry. Not every signer agrees fully with every statement in the text, and different members would undoubtedly emphasize different points in different ways. The very few instances in which there were divisions among us are explicitly described. But all of us affirm that the report reflects the consensus among us, and each of us subscribes to its overall content and thrust.

Executive Summary

The world's nuclear predicament has been formed by two interdependent factors:

— The nature and existence of nuclear weapons; and

— The profound distrust and antagonism embedded in the U.S.-Soviet relationship.

Each poses agonizing issues. Each constantly interacts with and affects the other. Neither can be dealt with independently of the other.

The Dilemma of Nuclear Weapons

Because of their nature—their enormous and instantaneous destructiveness and their aftereffects—nuclear weapons have profoundly changed the nature and meaning of warfare, and the risks and consequences of using force in international affairs. Traditional concepts and strategies are no longer adequate.

The central characteristic of this nuclear revolution is vulnerability. Both the Soviet Union and the United States have the means to destroy each other as a functioning society, and this mutual vulnerability is inescapable. The protection and survival of each depends on the restraint and cooperation of the other.

But if nuclear weapons have changed military and strategic realities, they have not changed human nature. Nations stubbornly cling to the power drives, egoisms and fears that have historically motivated nation-states, and obstinately resist abandoning traditional and conventional reasoning about politics and the use of force. Rather than change their thinking and behavior to reflect the realities of the nuclear revolution, nations still try to adapt those realities to old conventional ways and patterns. The implications and dilemmas of mutual vulnerability, moreover, are unfamiliar — and perhaps frightening.

The upshot has been persistent efforts to escape, deny, overcome or rationalize away the meaning of the nuclear revolution. Thus, there are those who argue that nuclear weapons can be made usable, and that limited nuclear war can therefore be contemplated and planned for; that a nation can achieve nuclear superiority with consequent political advantage; that defense technologies can render nuclear weapons impotent and obsolete; or that we should escape vulnerability simply by abolishing all nuclear weapons. But after studying and discussing these arguments, the committee concluded that all these arguments are ultimately futile efforts to escape the reality of mutual vulnerability.

The principal conclusions about nuclear weapons to which our inquiry led us may be summarized as follows:

- Nuclear weapons have no useful military role. Their use would be extremely difficult, if not impossible, to control. They generate risks out of all proportion to any rational goal.
- Mutual vulnerability cannot be escaped by building more and "better" weapons. Military "edges" or 'superiority" have no meaning in the nuclear era. The quest for nuclear superiority simply undermines the quest for nuclear security.
- The Strategic Defense Initiative ("Star Wars") offers virtually no prospect of achieving any of the visions that have given it momentum. It is extremely doubtful that SDI can ever become an effective shield protecting whole populations. It cannot unilaterally substitute a defensive strategy for deterrence; deployment of defensive systems by either side without comparable simultaneous deployment by the other would dangerously destabilize the strategic balance. Unrestrained pursuit of SDI will foreclose the opportunity to reduce strategic offensive forces. No agreement to reduce strategic offensive systems is possible without an agreement on defense; and without limits on offense, no effective defensive system is possible. Thus, whether the stated aim is to protect populations or enhance deterrence, the unilateral pursuit of SDI will inevitably trigger a dangerous new arms race in space.
- While the committee was drawn by the moral force behind the urge to abolish nuclear weapons, it recognized the practical problem of getting from here to there. A non-nuclear world cannot be achieved unilaterally or wishfully. It can come about only through mutual agreement and action over

time by all the nations possessing these weapons. A non-nuclear world should be our controlling vision, but we recognize that complete abolition is a future goal and not a present possibility.

The present situation is, hence, one of a nuclear impasse. The superpowers are at a standoff. Each possesses immensely powerful weapons, but cannot rationally use them. Mutual assured destruction is not a strategy. It is a condition. It is the very likely consequence of any significant nuclear exchange.

The essence of deterrence, then, is the probability of catastrophe if one side breaks the peace. That each superpower is deterred , however, is less the result of the other's explicit threat to inflict pain than it is, simply, the overwhelming sense of general danger which contemplation of nuclear weapons use produces. In a real sense deterrence inheres in the nature of the weapons.

It is important to understand deterrence in this "existential" sense, for deterrence is not a "thing" or an active agent. It is simply a mode of analysis, a way to explain the relationship between nuclear weapons and political decision-making. Weapons do not decide whether to be used or not; political leaders decide. The success or failure of deterrence therefore depends on the quality of political judgment.

The nuclear standoff is a source of stability in the sense that its deterrent effect does not depend on equal numbers and types of weapons, symmetries of force structures, or wavering perceptions of danger. Deterrence is not fragile.

At the same time, deterrence is not *automatically* stable. Nations can miscalculate. Accidents, misperceptions, irrational responses in the heat of crisis can all lead to a failure of deterrence. Deterrence can also be undermined by self-delusion should leaders talk themselves into believing that nuclear weapons can rationally be used, and that nuclear war can be limited and controlled.

Stability depends on mutual restraint in word and deed, prudence in the conduct of policy, and constant care not to send wrong signals to the other side. Stability in the international scene — in the military balance, in political and alliance relationships, in the level of tensions throughout the world — is a necessary condition for the maintenance of peace. Proposals for new weapons, changes in strategic doctrine, or political initiatives must be carefully assessed in the light of whether they will, or will not, contribute to this sense of stability.

To acknowledge the existence of mutual vulnerability and nuclear stalemate is *not* to argue that they constitute a satisfactory state of affairs or a preferential choice. Nor is it to argue that deterrence has no other form or scale than that which exists today. But mutual vulnerability and existential deterrence are basic conditions with which we must come to terms. We need also to understand that the primary way—perhaps the only way—out of dependence on the current balance of terror is through a steady modification and improvement of political relationships. There is no escape via technological fixes.

We have, thus, an urgent moral and political responsibility to use the relative stability of the current impasse to move toward a sturdier peace — and eventually a world freed from dependence on nuclear weapons. We need to move carefully in this regard, but with all deliberate speed.

The U.S.-Soviet Dilemma

While the enormous destructiveness of nuclear weapons makes the fact that they exist, in and of itself, a cause for terrible concern, what renders the danger acute is the fact that the two nations which possess nuclear arsenals of such size that they could destroy each other — and civilized society in the bargain — are also bitter antagonists. Nuclear issues, therefore, cannot be separated from U.S.-Soviet issues.

This dilemma may be summarized as follows:

The mutual vulnerability created by nuclear weapons means that the United States and the USSR share a common security whether they want to or not. Accommodation and coexistence are categorical imperatives resting on the inescapa-

14

ee concluded that agreements to control and
arsenals are central to a stable relationship be-
superpowers, and, therefore, to their mutual
hat the political path of seeking arms control
he only realistic and safe route to reduced de-
uclear weapons — and, eventually, to a non-

ee believes that arms control agreements should
ia: equivalence, reductions, stability and verifia-

and compliance are primarily political issues.
erification are a matter of weighing conflicting
ms control agreement poses some risks, but there
in not reaching agreements.
ential forum (known as the Standing Consulta-
ion) created by the SALT agreements to handle
uestions worked effectively through three previ-
rations. There is no intrinsic reason why it can-
to do so. Compliance problems are bound to be
ble during a period when U.S.-Soviet political re-
ained and each side questions the other's inten-
existing agreements. Therefore without a
olitical relationship that promotes compromise and
of existing agreements, the agreements will

gress in negotiations can be made if one side or
empts to resolve every detail at the outset. In our
amework" concept is the most practical procedure
progress and maintaining momentum. Agreement
work" need not await the fine print necessary for
greements. Subsequent "sub-limits" and specific
hammered out more easily within an agreed frame-
key to success is to sustain a long-term process that
series of mutually reinforcing strategic arms con-
ents.

18

ble reality that in a nuclear exchange everybody loses; in the final analysis they are the only rational and moral choices.

Yet the two nations are deeply divided — in philosophy, ideology, competing ambitions and national interests.

The distrust and sense of threat which Americans feel as a consequence are not without reason. Soviet leaders have been adversarial. Their purposes, methods and values are antithetical to ours. They confront us with formidable military power which undermines our sense of security. They demonstrate a continuing interest in expanding their global power and influence, whether motivated by communist ideology or nation-state imperialism. They suppress individual human rights and liberties both within their borders and wherever else they dominate.

In the aggregate, the Soviet Union presents us with an enduring challenge. It cannot be resolved to our satisfaction within the foreseeable future. The Soviet system is not going to collapse. We cannot subjugate or destroy it. We cannot change or convert it, we should nevertheless be able to meet that challenge without being obsessed by it. In the competition between us that will continue to go on around the world — in political, economic, ideological and power terms — many advantages lie with us. Not the least of these is the strength of our own values and principles.

Despite the rivalry, the two superpowers share a fundamental interest in avoiding nuclear war, and indeed in avoiding any direct military confrontation. Given the imperative of coexistence, we Americans are politically and morally required to build on this fundamental shared interest, and to find ways to manage our ongoing competition — to reduce its inherent risks and to make it more stable and predictable.

The task of accommodation and improving the U.S.-Soviet relationship is, of course, a two-way street. Misperception, erroneous perspectives and ethnocentric attitudes exist on both sides, and are equally harmful and counterproductive for both.

We find considerable hope, however, in recent indications that basic attitudes may be changing on the Soviet side. There

15

is now some evidence that the new Soviet leadership seeks to reduce some of the rigidity of the Soviet system and provide more room for diversity and creativity. Evidence also suggests that Gorbachev has concluded that nuclear weapons cannot be used to gain or preserve any valued political goal, that coexistence is in fact essential for the USSR. Certainly, as we issue this report, we find the environment for improved relations as propitious as it has ever been in the long history of US-Soviet competition.

While the the committee recognized that American efforts to improve the superpower relationship have to be matched from the Soviet side, it concentrated its study on what Americans can do because that is the area of action in which Americans can exercise control. For Americans to move toward breaking the cycle of antagonism and suspicion requires, we believe, at least three steps: 1) reaching a greater self-awareness of the mainsprings of our own national attitudes and behavior and the distorting effects of our own ethnocentricity and self-image; 2) achieving a balanced understanding of Soviet psychology, purposes, policies and methods; and 3) identifying and acting upon the elements of cooperation that can sustain constructive efforts on both sides.

Improvements in relationships and accommodations, and a more and balanced understanding and perception of the Soviet Union, will not resolve the basic conflict of purposes and values between us. But they can bring the conflict to a more rational level. Greater understanding and a mutual self awareness will also strip away the worst distorting myths and emotional fears. In time, a more trusting relationship may be established by a gradual process, in which every step contributes to the next.

The committee believes that certain American attitudes and "mind-sets" are needed, if we are to place our conflictive relationship on a rational basis:

- We should subscribe publicly to the principle of the inter-dependence of United States and Soviet security, the permanence of the nuclear impasse, the mutual suicide of nuclear weapons use, and the imperative of coexistence.

16

- We must understand
  values without de
  demonizing our adve
  are not to be mistaker
  ing out to reconcile
  ideals and principles.
- We need to acquire a re
  tion. This means more
  culture and language.
  curate an understandi
  feelings about us. In pr
  a)regular meetings bet
  and military leaders; b)
  and Soviet religious lea
  university programs in
  sive and intensive U.S.-S
  official and unofficial.
- We need to accord to the
  a world power, and to ac
  lion human beings as an e
  has nothing to do with m
  lence." It is a historical f
  American officials and citi
  need, and halt the conde
  sometimes demonstrate tc
  would do more to break the
  and distrust.

The members of the Comn
any of this will be easy, or that
be devoid of tension and ever
grounds for despair or for conc
ture cannot be different from t
the words of the American Cath
both our human potential for cr
tion in our midst which can ope
barely imagine."

The committ
reduce nuclear
tween the two
security; and t
agreements is
pendence on
nuclear world.

The commit
meet four crite
bility.

Verification
Questions of
risks. Every ar
are also risks

The confid
tive Commiss
compliance q
ous administ
not continue
more intracta
lations are st
tions towar
U.S.-Soviet p
reaffirmation
unravel.

Little pro
the other att
view, the "fr
for making
on a 'frame
follow-up a
rules can be
work. The
produces a
trol agreem

17

Our elected officials have a moral obligation and a political responsibility to reach arms control agreements that make the world a safer place. They should, accordingly, be held accountable for their performance in upholding this most essential of all public services. Until the American people consistently demand success in arms control from our elected officials, success will elude us. Nuclear arms control is not a matter of party politics; it is a national and moral imperative.

With regard to an arms control agenda, the committee believes that:

- We should move urgently toward an overall "framework" agreement which would cover deep reductions in strategic offensive forces, along the lines of the "Reykjavik framework."
- We should begin planning now for a series of follow-on agreements within that framework, such as were envisioned as follow-on reductions from the SALT II ceilings.
- We should proceed at a measured pace with a careful research program into defense technologies. But work on SDI should be in conformity with the established intent and purpose of the ABM Treaty. At the same time, however, we should seek to work out with the Soviet Union specific agreements on permissible SDI research under the ABM Treaty. The task should be not simply to stipulate a number of years for guaranteed ABM Treaty adherence, but to define how the treaty provisions might be applied to SDI research — and to Soviet space research — in a manner acceptable to both sides.
- We should agree to halt nuclear weapons testing underground as a concrete step toward negotiating a long overdue comprehensive test ban.
- We should announce our willingness to continue our moratorium on the testing of ASAT weapons against targets in space so long as the USSR exercises similar restraint.
- We should gradually reduce the flight testing of ICBMs and SLBM's.

- We should begin to destroy obsolete tactical nuclear weapons under appropriate safeguards, and invite international observers to witness the destruction.

The Moral and Religious Dimension

The traditional doctrine of "just war," part of early Christian thought, is applicable to, but inadequate for the nuclear age. The right of self-defense — and that extends to national defense — is recognized in Christian theology and tradition. We understand the perspective of Christian pacifism, and accept it as a personal option of individual conscience. We believe, however, that a distinction must be drawn between pacifism as a personal option, and pacifism as public policy. Most of the committee do not support the latter.

Similarly, we recognize as legitimate the perspective of non-violent resistance, and accept it as a personal option. We are honestly troubled, however, by the claim that non-violent resistance can be effective in settling conflicts between nations. We have difficulty seeing how it meets the responsibility to protect the innocent from external aggression, although we understand it as a valid, and sometimes feasible, means of resisting internal oppression and injustice.

The committee recognizes the paradox that on the one hand we believe that to use nuclear weapons would be morally wrong, yet we propose that we should continue to possess them because of their existential and inevitable deterrent effect. We take this view because we see no other acceptable way to reduce the likelihood of nuclear war at this time. We believe we are bound by the logic of mutual vulnerability and existential deterrence, and cannot escape it or survive by acting as if it did not exist.

We realize that there are moral ambiguities here. For some members of the committee, this position is the lesser evil; for others a moral responsibility in a broken world; for still others an interim necessity on a course toward the abolition of nuclear weapons; and for all, the recognition that there are no sinless policies in a sinful world.

None of the committee's members could imagine any circumstances in which deliberately initiating the use of nuclear weapons could be morally justified. For we do not believe that their use could terminate a conventional conflict, nor preclude a nuclear exchange once one side had used nuclear weapons.

We were divided, however, over the issue of retaliatory or second use. Some felt they could not exclude the possibility that some particular, limited U.S. response might prevent a greater evil — e.g., might halt an escalation to total war. Others felt that nuclear weapons, being intrinsically evil, must not be used under any circumstances.

As already noted, to argue that deterrence is necessary, is not to argue that it is desirable, or that it must be permanent. The current task before us, both morally and prudentially, is to move away from dependence on nuclear deterrence — while recognizing its current necessity — to a world without nuclear weapons.

For Christians the problem of relations with the USSR is especially sharp and poignant because it juxtaposes the drives and self-love of human nature with a principle that is at the heart of our Christian faith: the obligation to love and be reconciled with our enemies. Christ's redemptive ministry, it seems clear to us, compels us to accept reconciliation as an essential element of our "controlling vision" in public policy, however antagonistic and intractable our adversaries may be.

For Christians, this compulsion lies in our belief in the transcendence of God, the fact that humans are the clearest reflection of God's presence in the world, and the biblical proclamation that in Christ we are neither Jew nor Greek, but all one in Him. For these things provide the sense of universal community that can underpin the policy ethic and statecraft of reconciliation that is required for survival in the nuclear era.

* * * * * *

As we seek to demonstrate in this report, peace in the nuclear age is a multi-dimensional issue. On a military level of analysis, our controlling vision is a world without nuclear weapons. On a political level of analysis, our vision is a world of peace with a policy ethic of justice and a sense of community. But for us Christians, the most profound hope is on the theological level, for here the analysis directly concerns the issues of human nature, Christ's redemption of the world, and God's will.

According to biblical witness, we are flawed in our nature and will always exhibit a measure of selfishness and folly, as well as a measure of self-sacrifice and good judgment. Nonetheless, we believe our destiny is not determined by these limitations, nor by the principles of economic theory and practice, technological development or political pressure. We deeply and steadfastly believe that we have a sufficient measure of free choice to avoid self-destruction. This report was written in that religious faith.

It is not given to us to discern the shape of our future, but we are called to be a people of hope and not of fear. Nor can we know the exact kind of governance that will be required in the decades ahead to keep the peace in a nuclear world. But as each future comes to us, our challenge will be the same — to act justly and deal righteously as God gave us the wisdom and courage so to do. The final disposition of our hope for a true peace lies, not in our human abilities, but in the God who not only takes and uses our strengths, but who also redeems our weaknesses and sin.

Chapter I
INTRODUCTION
TO OUR INQUIRY

The world's nuclear predicament has been shaped by two sets of factors which constantly interact and affect each other:

— The nature and presence of nuclear weapons; and

— The profound distrust and antagonism embedded in the U.S.-Soviet relationship.

The horrors held out by nuclear weapons have been graphically described many times and need not be repeated here. What is clear is that the existence and nature of nuclear weapons — their enormous and instantaneous destructiveness and their after-effects — have profoundly changed the nature and meaning of warfare, the risks and consequences of using force in international affairs and traditional concepts and rules of strategy. Nuclear weapons can simply not be "conventionalized" either in our thinking or in use.

While the enormous destructiveness of these weapons makes the fact that they exist in and of itself a cause for terrible concern, what renders the danger acute is the fact that the only two nations which possess nuclear arsenals of such size that they can destroy each other — and civilized society in the bargain — are also bitter antagonists. The profound distrust and antagonism which divide the two superpowers are deeply rooted in the conflict of values and purposes between the American and Soviet societies. Nuclear issues, therefore, cannot be separated from U.S.-Soviet issues. Indeed, the positions most Americans take on nuclear questions tend to be determined by their perception of the nature and goals of the Soviet Union.

Both the Soviet Union and the United States find themselves caught in a terrible dilemma. On the one hand, they want to avoid a nuclear holocaust. On the other, however, they feel driven by fear and mistrust to maintain and strengthen their nuclear arsenals. Both remain trapped, as it were, in national attitudes and illusions. To paraphrase one of our witnesses, each fears nuclear weapons in the hands of the other "more than it fears the weapons in the abstract."[1]

We believe, therefore, that the crux of the nuclear dilemma lies in the state of the relationship between the superpowers. It is also clear that improving that relationship is a two-way street. Misperception, erroneous perspectives and ethnocentric attitudes exist on both sides.

In this country, public concern about nuclear weapons and potential nuclear conflict is widespread. Our deference in earlier years to self-proclaimed "experts" — government officials, defense intellectuals, military strategists—has now given way to an increasing concern and claim that we should have a voice in nuclear policy. With this concern has come a growing sense that governments and their policies are failing to control the danger. Despite the Iceland summit, the arms build-up continues, tensions between nations increase, and confrontation sharpens. It is this perception of policy drift that lies at the root of our apprehension.

In the coming months and years, the United States government — and by extension, the American people — will face a number of specific decisions with regard to relations with the Soviets, nuclear weapons systems and arms control negotiations. Such piecemeal decisions, however, often affect the whole range of future choices, foreclosing some, altering others, and shaping future circumstances. The decision to place more than one nuclear warhead atop a ballistic missile, for example, changed the basic nature of the nuclear problem. Public debate in the future will need to focus on complex decisions about

[1] Roger Shinn, "A Dilemma, Seen from Several Sides," *Christianity and Crisis*, January 18, 1982, p 373.

nuclear weapons and space, and the choices we make will shape the international nuclear issue for the next generation. The American people thus face something of a "ticking clock" with respect to a whole range of crucial decisions regarding weapons and negotiating strategies. Wrong choices may produce not only dangerous, but possibly irreversible, results. Much rests, therefore, on the quality of judgment used and the wisdom shown in reaching these decisions.

Despite this, however, many people who are concerned about nuclear weapons still hesitate to confront these issues directly. They may feel that the topic is too technical and complex for the average person to understand. Or they may believe that ordinary citizens can not influence policy decisions even when they do understand the issues. We believe that neither of these reasons is valid.

First, the issue of nuclear war is too important to be left to experts. In any case, there are no "nuclear war experts" in the sense of someone having certain knowledge. All views are guesses, deductions, opinions. Strategies rest on tenuous webs of assumptions. Persons who have run computer simulations know how artificial their input numbers are. But if the issues are complex, they are not incomprehensible. We can understand what is at stake, and what the choices are. The decisions that have to be made are not basically scientific. They are political. The problems of nuclear war are not essentially technical. They are human. The nuclear question contains issues of security, politics, human nature, morality. There is, moreover, a plethora of material available, and it is easily gathered. What is important is that each of us study and *think* about this issue.

Secondly, we are not — and must not become—passive objects of nuclear policy formulated by others. We are actors in this drama, and our opinion can influence our government's policy through the democratic process. Indeed, all citizens bear ultimate responsibility for those policies since we are a government of, by and for the people. We were particularly struck by the Harvard Nuclear Study Group's comments about citizen involvement in the nuclear debate. The group points out that elected officials, who in this country make the final decisions about security policy, are themselves also lay people. They are not unlike most of us. They have not spent long years learning the technical details of weapons systems, nor are they experts on strategy, treaties, verification or other nuclear fine points. The American elected official listens to various opinions about the alternative policies and then, within his or her ability, decides what is best for the nation. "The citizen's task is no more and no less."[2]

The problems which the nuclear dilemma poses for the Christian conscience are also rooted in the two interacting poles of that issue — the nature of the weapons and the antagonism between the superpowers. There is clearly no parallel between past wars and the use of force and the use of *nuclear* force. The potential for catastrophic destruction inherent in the nature of nuclear weapons and the fact that no nation can be sure that their use can be limited, discriminate or controlled pose the issue that their use would be an offense against the doctrine of creation, i.e. usurpation of the sole prerogative of the Creator.

Aside from the question of physical survival, the nuclear dilemma also gives rise to questions that stem from the very roots of Christian morality — How should we, as followers of Christ, love an enemy? To what extent may one defend one's life, one's standards, values, society, or country with force? If physical survival and the preservation of our national and political values are not the supreme ends of human life, is it still not just and moral to defend them? Is there a difference between the individual expression of the ethic of loving one's enemy and the collective political expression of nation-states dealing with adversary states?

These are subtle and complicated questions, and they are not new. But never has the moral dimension of such questions been more compelling and urgent, since nuclear issues touch

---

[2] Harvard Nuclear Study Group, *Living With Nuclear Weapons*. New York: Bantam Books, 1983., pp 9-11.

so extensively and intensely the full spectrum of human lives. Indeed, it is precisely the fact that the problems of nuclear war are basically rooted not in technical factors but in the human impulses of power-seeking, national rivalries and pride that makes the church and its teachings relevant to our condition. Christ's teachings, we submit, offer effective and realistic insights with which to understand and deal with human nature, and hence to comprehend and cope with the problems confronting us. It is precisely the insights and concepts of Christianity's biblical vision of the world which provide us with the hope of working our way out of the cruel dilemmas we face. Christ, in His ministry, illustrated the nature of God's love for the world, and His concern for justice, mercy and peace. Christ calls us to be agents of those purposes in our lives. We support the concept of individual prophetic witness, and the responsibility of Christian communities to speak and teach through their leaders.

We conclude, therefore, that the obligation to enter into the nuclear debate springs not only from the urgent responsibilities of citizenship, but also compellingly from the nature of our Christian faith. Church people have both the right and the obligation to get into this discussion, and their moral and biblical witness has never been more greatly needed than now.

It is a common human habit, especially in debates on ideological questions, to assume that opposition to one's own position means that the opponent is *ipso facto* at the opposite pole. People are tempted to believe there is no valid middle ground between opposing poles, or any room for ambiguity. In the nuclear debate, for example, we encounter the sentiments that if one opposes the arms race then one must be advocating disarmament; or, that one cannot oppose the Soviet Union and at the same time favor diminishing the U.S. nuclear arsenal; or, that favoring a strong defense means favoring militarism and nuclear war fighting; or, that opposing communism means one cannot reach an accommodation with the Soviet Union.

But the more we have studied the more we have learned that nuclear realities do not present such simplistic, stark either/or constructions. The debate does not distill to "Better Red than Dead." It contains complexities, a middle ground between these opposing extremes and, even, paradox.

The desire for national security for all people, for example, is a valid and necessary concept that must be taken into account. But we err if we see the search for national security as a zero-sum proposition that states: If one side gains, the other side loses. Such cherished goods as peace and security are gained or lost by all sides together. Even so practiced a geostrategist as Henry Kissinger once observed: "...the quest for total security for some turns into insecurity for the remainder. Stability depends on the relative satisfaction and therefore the relative dissatisfaction of the various states. The pursuit of peace must therefore begin with a pragmatic concept of co-existence — especially in a period of ideological conflict."[3]

Thus our inquiry, spurred by considerations such as those outlined above, concentrated in effect on the two horns of the nuclear dilemma:

— What are nuclear weapons for?

— How should the United States and the Soviet Union deal with each other?

The following chapter describes the history of the nuclear arms race and the nuclear debate to see how we got to where we are, and to establish the setting for the following discussion. Chapter 3 examines the question of nuclear weapons and mutual vulnerability. Chapter 4 looks at the question of U.S.-Soviet relations, and Chapter 5 deals with the point at which these two dimensions come together most compellingly — arms control negotiations. Chapter 6 discusses the religious and moral dimensions of all these questions. We close with some final thoughts in an epilogue.

---

[3] Address delivered to the *Pacem in Terris III* Conference, Washington, D.C., October 8, 1973. Text as printed in Henry Kissinger, *American Foreign Policy*, expanded edition, New York: W.W. Norton & Cox, 1974, p 259.

Chapter II
SETTING FOR POLICY CHOICES

The arsenals of the United States and the Soviet Union contain approximately 50,000 nuclear weapons. When these weapons were first conceived and produced, no one imagined that inventories would reach such levels. Yet the competition in nuclear armaments has not slackened. Today, it is as vigorous as ever.

Both nations continue to press ahead with "modernization" programs that more than compensate for the retirement of weapons that were produced a generation ago.

This build-up reflects a series of choices made by political leaders in Washington and Moscow. The result of these choices has been increasingly sophisticated weapons and capabilities for destruction, and a diminishing sense of security in both nations. The committee, therefore, began its inquiry into this spiraling condition by asking: How did we get here?

The committee reviewed the history of the arms race. Then we turned to deterrence as part of our consideration of the nature and meaning of these nuclear weapons systems. Both are presented in that order here. Indeed, we do not believe that deterrence can be accurately understood except in this context, even though it is generally treated as if it were a discrete body of doctrine or strategy.

The History
During World War II, at great expense and urgency, the United States developed the atomic bomb in the belief that Nazi

Germany was pursuing the same objective. Germany was defeated before its team of scientists made much headway and before the U.S. A-bomb was ready. There was no slackening of effort in the Manhattan Project, however, and shortly after Germany's surrender the United States readied two atomic bombs which were used against Japan as an alternative to a costly invasion by U.S. ground forces of the Japanese home islands. The Secretary of War at the time, Henry L. Stimson, defended the decision to drop the bombs as "the least abhorrent choice."

In 1949, the Soviet Union exploded its first atomic bomb, and President Truman decided to push ahead with development of a U.S. hydrogen weapon. His decision was driven by fears that the Soviet Union was also working on its own hydrogen weapon, and indeed one year after the United States exploded the first hydrogen bomb in 1952, the Soviet Union matched the achievement. Both nations thus acquired the power to unleash the equivalent of millions of tons of TNT with a single explosion. In contrast, the bomb that destroyed Hiroshima had the equivalent of 13,000 tons of TNT.

Both nations also undertook development of delivery systems for their nuclear weapons, to reach targets several thousand miles away. Initially, each side chose to mate its weapons with bombers — an area of the competition in which the United States had steadily gained a decided advantage. By the mid-1950s, however, that advantage was questioned by American officials suspicious of Soviet intentions. The appearance of new combat aircraft in the Soviet Union, combined with an inadequate means of assessing the extent of Soviet aircraft production, led to claims of a "bomber gap." While President Eisenhower rejected these assertions, he nonetheless accelerated production of U.S. bombers, and authorized development of two new means of delivering nuclear weapons: intercontinental and submarine-launched ballistic missiles (ICBMs and SLBMs).

Meanwhile, first the British, then the French and later the Chinese governments set out to build, develop and deploy their own nuclear weapons. Other countries are suspected of following suit. While nuclear arsenals other than the Soviet and American remained small, they complicated the international nuclear equation as it developed during the 1960s and 1970s.

Washington and Moscow began to cooperate in the early 1960s to prevent the acquisition of nuclear arms by other countries. Throughout the 1950s and the following decade, the United States and the Soviet Union continued along parallel tracks of nuclear weapons development, with the United States seemingly in the lead. Most Americans, therefore, were surprised when in 1957 the Soviets launched a small satellite by means of a rocket—a rocket that was seen as the harbinger of Soviet capability to propel a hydrogen bomb over intercontinental distances. "Sputnik," the Soviet rocket, led to claims of a "missile gap," which became a political issue that helped elect John F. Kennedy to the presidency in 1960. That gap, like the "bomber gap" before it, proved illusory. The Soviets were indeed building missiles by the late 1950s, but they were intermediate-range ballistic missiles (IRBMs) targeted on Europe, not intercontinental ballistic missiles capable of striking targets in the United States.

Nevertheless, Sputnik did become the spur for a large and sustained U.S. effort to develop its own strategic missiles. By 1959, the United States began deploying ICBMs and, by 1962, SLBMs. The process resulted in the deployment of some 1000 Minutemen ICBMs and 41 missile-carrying submarines. The Soviets matched, and raised: They exceeded the number of U.S. missile launchers by the early 1970s.

One reason for the Soviet missile buildup was their perceived need to compensate for the decision by the United States to forego additional missile launchers, and instead place more than one warhead atop U.S. ballistic missiles. These warheads could be directed at separate targets—in effect, making a single missile able to destroy several widely dispersed targets. This technique is known as "MIRVing," the acronym for Multiple, Independently Targetable Reentry Vehicle.

The technological possibilities of MIRVs were first explored in the late 1960s, at a time when U.S. intelligence agencies believed the Soviets were developing anti-missile defenses. The MIRV development made the prospects for a successful anti-ballistic missile (ABM) defense seem very dim. Since a defense of cities must be perfect to be effective, and since multiple warhead missiles — MIRVed missiles — seemed likely to overwhelm any defense system, how could a nation defend itself? MIRVs were promoted in the United States for two primary reasons: as a means to penetrate Soviet defenses; and as a counter offsetting the build-up in Soviet ICBMs, thus maintaining an advantageous U.S. position at least cost. When the Soviet Union also deployed MIRVs in the mid-1970s, this advantage was lost. But in the process, the strategic arsenals of both sides climbed several fold, maintaining the strategic stalemate at higher levels. The U.S. and the Soviet Union continue to deploy new ICBMs, SLBMs, bombers, advanced cruise missiles and intermediate-range nuclear forces like the SS-20 and Pershing II missiles.

While building nuclear weapons capabilities, both nations also took steps toward arms control. The first important post-World War II initiative for disarmament was the Baruch Plan, which called for the complete elimination of nuclear weapons and for international control over the mining and production of fissionable materials such as uranium, used in the construction of nuclear weapons. The Baruch Plan called for international control first, then disarmament. The Soviet Union objected, and put forward a different proposal. The Soviets called first for disarmament, and then international control but without adequate verification. The United States objected to this proposal, and stalemate ensued. Both nations continued to offer proposals for general and complete disarmament during the next 15 years, but they produced no meaningful negotiations.

The first significant accomplishment in strategic arms control came in 1963, when the United States, Great Britain, and the Soviet Union signed a Limited Test Ban Treaty. This barred nuclear weapon tests in the atmosphere, outer space, and underwater; the treaty was "limited" because it still permitted underground nuclear weapon tests. In 1969, the two nuclear powers began negotiations to restrict strategic forces. By 1972, the Strategic Arms Limitation Talks (SALT) yielded two agreements: the Anti-Ballistic Missile (ABM) Treaty, ratified by the Senate, which limited strategic defenses, and the Interim Agreement, which limited offensive nuclear forces. The ABM Treaty allowed each side to defend two separate locations within each nation. Later, this was reduced to a single site per side.

The Interim Agreement froze the number of missile launchers then in place or under construction. It did not prohibit modernization programs, such as MIRVs — a limitation neither side was prepared to accept.

In 1979, the U.S. and USSR negotiators agreed to the SALT II Treaty, which generated heated debates within the United States, and was withdrawn by the Administration before it was brought to a Senate vote. To some critics, the agreement seemed too modest because it failed to provide for any real arms reduction. To others, it failed to deal with the threat of a new missile gap, which they now saw arising from a steady increase in new land-based Soviet ICBMs. Russian support for leftist movements around the globe — especially in Angola and Ethiopia — also troubled many Senators, and the Soviet invasion of Afghanistan in 1979 sealed the treaty's fate. In addition, there were numerous charges of inequities in the agreement and difficulties in verifying its provisions, along with complaints about Soviet noncompliance with the SALT I accords.

While agreeing to abide by the terms of both SALT accords negotiated by his predecessors, President Ronald Reagan made clear his preference for a different tactic in subsequent arms control negotiations. He proposed deep cuts in land-based missiles, which are the largest and most threatening component of Soviet nuclear forces. Two sets of talks were established: the Strategic Arms Reduction Talks (START), as SALT was renamed, and the Intermediate-range Nuclear Forces (INF) negotiations, designed to deal with shorter-range missiles such as the Soviet

SS-20, the U.S. Pershing II, and ground-launched cruise missiles (GLCMs). But the Reagan Administration offered little by way of trade-offs to secure mutually advantageous agreements, and the Soviets also offered one-sided negotiating positions.

After the first cruise missiles and Pershing IIs were deployed in Europe in December, 1983, the Soviet Union suspended the START and INF talks. By March 1985, however, the two superpowers had resumed negotiations in three interrelated segments: strategic nuclear forces; intermediate range forces; and space weapons. The differences between the two sides, however, were wider than ever. The Russians again took a hard line against deployment of missiles in Europe and retracted some of the bargaining concessions they had made before their walkout more than a year earlier. They declared a readiness to negotiate deep cuts in nuclear weapons, but only after the Reagan Administration renounced its Strategic Defense Initiative or 'Star Wars." The U.S. delegation expressed its readiness to negotiate deep cuts in offensive forces, but an unwillingness to do more than "discuss" strategic defenses and the transition from an offensive-dominated nuclear world to a defensive one.

Both sides also faced decisions about the SALT I Interim Agreement and the SALT II Treaty's limits on offensive forces. SALT I had expired in 1977, and SALT II in 1985. Political leaders on both sides questioned the other's willingness to show restraint and to comply with these agreements. The Reagan Administration published lists of what it saw as Soviet noncompliance problems with previous agreements, and expressed fears that the Soviets intended to abrogate the ABM treaty. The Kremlin pointed to the conflict between the "Star Wars" initiative and the existing ABM Treaty, the unprecedented increases in U.S. defense spending and the publicly-voiced Reagan administration skepticism toward new arms control agreements.

Despite the common threat of nuclear war, and the prospect of more menacing war fighting capabilities on both sides, neither the Soviets nor the Americans have been able to agree on formulas to reduce strategic nuclear forces although an agreement on INF now appears likely. Compliance questions have been increasingly difficult to resolve privately, as first the United States and then the Soviet Union issued reports charging violations of arms control agreements by the other side.

One area where the superpowers have cooperated is in nuclear non-proliferation; that is, the acquisition of nuclear weapons by additional countries. Both the Soviets and Americans worked together to produce the Non-Proliferation Treaty (NPT) in 1968. The NPT is essentially a compact between nuclear and non-nuclear weapon states. The nuclear-weapons nations have pledged to prevent the spread of nuclear weapons and to reduce the weapons in their arsenals, while promoting the peaceful uses of nuclear energy in non-weapon states. Many non-weapon nations have pledged not to develop or acquire nuclear weapons, and to accept "safeguards" against the diversion of fissionable material produced in their nuclear reactors for military purposes. In 1957, the International Atomic Energy Agency was created to conduct inspections of civilian nuclear power plants, and to implement other safeguards.

In Article VI of the NPT, the United States and the Soviet Union pledged to negotiate an early halt to the nuclear arms race, and then to work toward nuclear disarmament. To put it mildly, they have completely failed to live up to this treaty obligation.

Some think that the NPT has worked reasonably well, since the number of nuclear weapon states is lower today than most experts originally predicted. However, China and France are not parties to the treaty, nor are six "near nuclear weapon" states (Argentina, Brazil, India, Israel, Pakistan, South Africa). Non-nuclear weapons states, however, strongly criticize the superpowers for not reducing their deployed nuclear forces, and many of them charge that the nuclear states want to keep a monopoly of nuclear technology for commercial use.

Despite common concerns about proliferation, disagreements persist over how to avoid further nuclear proliferation. Interestingly enough, unlike other aspects of the nuclear question, arguments over non-proliferation policy have tended to be more contentious among allies (over questions of sales and exports of nuclear technology) and between political parties in the United States (over military assistance), than between the two superpowers.

Deterrence

Each superpower has long justified the possession of nuclear weapons in order to deter aggressive action, including nuclear weapons use, by the other. The term "deterrence" has come to embrace a wide range of meanings, and has been used to justify many different policies, weapons programs, and strategies.

In the brief period of U.S. nuclear monopoly, deterrence strategy was relatively straightforward: If the Soviet Union tried to overrun Western Europe, the United States would inflict "unacceptable" punishment by atomic air strikes. When the Soviet Union also acquired a stockpile of nuclear weapons, deterrence strategy became more complicated. Although U.S. war plans still stressed devastating nuclear attacks on Russian territory, there was no longer assurance that such strikes could be carried out without provoking major counterstrikes against the United States. U.S. leaders began to realize they were now in a situation of mutual vulnerability which required a rethinking of the U.S. strategic position.

It is important to note that since the founding of the North Atlantic Alliance over 35 years ago, the United States has given its nuclear protection to our European allies. The solidarity of the Alliance has in fact depended to a very large degree upon this "extended deterrence" — the willingness of the United States to protect with its nuclear weapons not only Chicago or Omaha, but also Hamburg, Paris, Brussels, and London. Behind this commitment was the assessment that the Western Allies could not win a conventional, non-nuclear war against the larger Soviet and Warsaw Pact forces. The United States has always predicated much of its nuclear strategy and weapons procurement on countering what it thought, at least during the 1950s and 1960s, was the most likely cause of Soviet-U.S. war: a Soviet invasion of Western Europe.

On the assumption that Soviet strategic forces would continue to grow, U.S. leaders wrestled with the requirements for deterrence in these new circumstances. In 1962, Secretary of Defense Robert McNamara developed the doctrine of "assured destruction." According to this doctrine, the U.S. must maintain sufficient nuclear forces to destroy large segments of Soviet industry and population in the event of a Soviet attack; if it did so, the Soviets would refrain from attacking — i.e., would be deterred. This concept, which acquired the acronym MAD (for "mutual assured destruction") had a strong impact on official and public thinking about nuclear strategy during the 1960s and early 1970s. Secretary McNamara's primary purpose was to limit the growth of strategic nuclear weapons by seeking to demonstrate that a finite and relatively low number of weapons (about 400) was needed to "assure destruction" of the Soviet Union and thus prevent nuclear war.

During the 1970s, critics alleged that MAD was no longer a credible deterrent because the Soviets were developing nuclear weapons that could arrive quickly and accurately against U.S. military targets. Destroying Soviet cities in response, this argument went, would be suicidal since American cities would then be attacked. Moreover, being suicidal, the threat would not deter lower levels of Soviet violence. If the United States could respond to a Soviet move only by resorting to all-out war, the critics continued, then the Russians might undertake a limited attack, leaving the United States with only the options of suicide or surrender. Therefore, the argument concluded, the United States needed more flexible military options that would allow it to meet a variety of Soviet challenges with a variety of responses, including a limited nuclear response to a Soviet conventional attack.

Despite the popular impression that the MAD strategy was directed exclusively at industrial and population targets, researchers who have seen recently declassified U.S. targeting plans have concluded that these plans continued to include military targets.

There has always been a gap between the public debate on nuclear strategy and the secret work of the military war planners. There is the public arena of debate among defense intellectuals, academics, political leaders, strategists, and government officials. But there is also the classified activity of professional military officers. Their specific task is to formulate options for how weapons will be used and what targets will be hit. For decades, military targets have been at the top of the list. However, given the proximity of many Soviet military targets to urban centers, no effort to limit the effects of a nuclear attack to one category of target or another could succeed as a practical matter.

The divergence is still great today between public statements and actual military planning. While the U.S. and Soviet leaders talk about there being no winners in a nuclear war, defense planners on both sides appear to be going about their business while continuing to build forces that, to put it charitably, signify a clear desire not to *lose* in nuclear exchanges. Whatever the public statements of U.S. or Soviet leaders, defense planners continue to update lists of targets and plans for a wide range of contingencies.

Throughout the 1970s, official U.S. policy shifted the interpretation of deterrence to mean not only punishment, but also "denial" of any Soviet gains or objectives. This policy was an effort to convince the Soviets that the United States had the power to defeat any limited attack or probe they might make, and thus dissuade them from trying to achieve any gain or political advantage by arms, however limited. This distinction is important to us because deterrence by denial requires nuclear war-fighting or "counterforce" capabilities—nuclear forces that could be used accurately and selectively against Soviet military targets at varying levels of "controlled" violence. In contrast, the objective of assured destruction does not require a large inventory of highly accurate nuclear warheads.

Secretary of Defense James Schlesinger took the lead in pushing for more flexibility and nuclear options in order to deter Soviet aggression and to deny Soviet objectives in the event of a military confrontation. This meant increased emphasis on counterforce capabilities. In the Carter administration this became known as the "countervailing strategy." The Reagan administration has gone beyond a strategy of nuclear deterrence based on denial of Soviet war-fighting objectives. An official planning document, leaked to the press, called for nuclear forces able to "prevail" in nuclear exchanges, even protracted ones.[1]

Supporters of the concept of assured destruction disapproved of the trends in U.S. nuclear war planning and projected increases in U.S. nuclear war-fighting capabilities. They argued that MAD was not a theory; it was an inevitable fact of life in the event of nuclear war. But the buildup of Soviet nuclear war-fighting capabilities after the SALT I accords, signed in 1972, strengthened the position of those advocating similar U.S. counterforce weapons.

This capsule summary of deterrence theory indicates a progressive blurring of the line between deterrence and use.

Why is it that elaborate theories of deterrence by means of nuclear war-fighting capabilities have gained such ground, leading to offensive forces well beyond levels required for assured retaliation? The answer lies, in our view, in muddled thinking that continues to look at nuclear weapons in conventional ways, and refuses to accept the logic of mutual vulnerability.

[1] Richard Halloran, "Pentagon Draws Up First Strategy for Fighting A Long Nuclear War," *The New York Times*, May 30, 1982, p. A1.

Chapter III
MUTUAL VULNERABILITY:
THE PARADOX OF DETERRENCE

In 1946, Albert Einstein stated: "The unleashed power of the atom has changed everything save our way of thinking, and thus we drift toward unparalleled catastrophe." Nuclear weapons have indeed rendered traditional concepts of warfare and strategy inadequate and misleading. The simple fact is that the United States has the means to destroy the Soviet Union as a functioning society, and the Soviet Union has the means to destroy the United States. This mutual vulnerability is inescapable. It is an existential condition. An entire "logic" of mutual vulnerability can be derived from these circumstances. Its axioms may be stated as follows:

1. Nuclear weapons exist.
2. They are immensely, almost unimaginably, destructive.
3. They are possessed by both superpowers in such numbers and in such forms that they cannot be destroyed in a preemptive surprise attack.
4. There is no way to shelter entire societies from them.

It follows from these axioms that, in a direct confrontation between the superpowers, both civilizations are inescapably at risk. *Any* violence between the United States and the Soviet Union could spill over into nuclear devastation. Neither superpower can enjoy the kind or degree of security that was available to it in pre-nuclear days. Security itself has become mutual. The protection and survival of each nation depends on the restraint and cooperation of the other.

Security is found in mutual restraint: that peculiar, strained co-existence imposed and dictated to the nuclear powers by the nuclear arsenals. Although strategists of both sides may calculate in exquisite detail each side's relative strengths — debating throw-weights versus warheads, and measuring land-based, sea-launched, and air-borne weapons in varying ways — the central, unalterable fact that has restrained the superpowers through 40 years of competition has been the risk of nuclear devastation and the condition of mutual vulnerability.

It is not surprising that people resist the logic of mutual vulnerability. Its implications and dilemmas are frightening, and unfamiliar. To Americans, for example, the precept that their security depends ultimately on the restraint and cooperation of Russians is a notion that they may instinctively wish to reject. No doubt Russians react similarly from their perspective. The logic of mutual vulnerability means that Americans (and Russians) cannot assure their security solely on the basis of their own strength. Yet such a conclusion contradicts what we have always accepted as "common sense."

There is something alien and seemingly perverse in the idea that peace is preserved by a military stalemate that puts millions of innocent people in mortal peril. Thus the concept of mutual vulnerability and the deterrent effect which derives from it are persistently attacked as militarily unacceptable and morally abhorrent. Yet given the reality of the superpowers' nuclear arsenals, the danger of mutual destruction cannot be erased.

As a consequence, the committee found that much of the policy debates, strategic theorizing and public discussion about nuclear weapons and strategy reflect efforts to escape, deny or overcome the logic of mutual vulnerability.

In our inquiry, the committee heard and read the arguments of experts who denied the validity of the axioms above, or who argued that their terms could be altered. As we detail here, some challenge the first axiom — that nuclear weapons exist — by saying that we can and must urgently do away with them, reject them, dismantle them, and refuse to depend on them.

42

Others attack the second axiom — that nuclear weapons are immensely destructive — by arguing that small and accurate nuclear weapons can be built and used in such a way as to fall within the range of conventional weapons. These weapons, they argue, could be used the way conventional weapons have always been used: to fight wars for specific political objectives, or to force a war to a conclusion on favorable terms. The implication is that nuclear war need not be particularly catastrophic, and can therefore be contemplated and planned for.

Other experts attack the third axiom — that preemptive attack cannot escape retaliation — by arguing that a low-risk first strike attack may soon be possible. Finally, there are those who challenge the last axiom by holding out the vision that technology can provide a protective shield for the peoples of the United States and their allies, if we will but take up the scientific challenge.

The committee understands the allure of all these positions. It is, after all, difficult to be satisfied with the idea that the greatest peril in human history has to be managed in terms of mutual vulnerabilities. It is hard to grasp Winston Churchill's paradox that "safety is the sturdy child of terror." But after studying and discussing the arguments, we conclude that the challenges to these axioms are ultimately futile efforts to escape the reality of mutual vulnerability.

We call these challenges "escapes" for they seem to be motivated by a psychological need to deny the inescapable fact of mutual vulnerability, to find exits where there are none.

The Escape Into Abolition

Given the horrible nature of nuclear weapons, it is understandable that some people seek to escape the nuclear danger by simply advocating abolition of the weapons. Proposals for the abolition of nuclear weapons cover a broad range of beliefs — from nuclear pacifism to complex proposals for disarmament. Most contemplate various kinds of disarmament actions and geopolitical changes which would make nuclear weapons unneeded.

Few people today advocate unilateral disarmament. As one of our witnesses has written:

> In the present state of fear and distrust, neither of the great powers will, by any act of choice, make itself vulnerable to the other. And even as a matter of theological and ethical theory, I do not think such an action [unilateral disarmament] desirable. It would not enhance the peace of the world. The one situation more dangerous and more fraught with injustice than a balance of terror is a monopoly of terror.[1]

Many do argue, however, for what has been called the "snowball effect." Deep cuts, by mutual agreement or unilateral example, would engender confidence and goodwill between the superpowers, lead to other cuts, more goodwill and so forth down to zero. Jonathan Schell has described what he called "weaponless deterrence" — i.e., the nuclear nations sign a pact scrapping their weapons, but keep factories poised to resume production. This, Schell argues, would be protection against cheating, since each would know that others could reestablish a retaliatory force by resuming production. Still others see disarmament made safe through world government or some other form of multilateral governance.

An assumption implicit in virtually all of these proposals is that nuclear weapons are the main cause of antagonism and friction between the superpowers; hence if they were removed, relations would greatly improve. As we note in chapter IV, we believe that the antagonisms between the United States and the Soviet Union are ideological and deep, and that the fundamental danger of war lies in the adversarial nature of that relationship, not in the size and shape of nuclear weapons.

The summit meeting at Reykjavik, in which the possibility of scrapping all nuclear weapons in a foreseeable future was discussed, reopened questions that need to be pondered. One is whether a world without nuclear weapons would in fact be a safer world. The pro-nuclear argument is that, if the super-

---

[1] Shinn, *op. cit.*, "A Dilemma, Seen From Several Sides", p 14.

powers scrap their nuclear weapons, then conventional war between them would be more likely, since it is the danger of nuclear war — which neither can control — that now restrains them from confrontation. Moreover this argument holds that, since it is impossible to eradicate the knowledge of how to make nuclear weapons, the temptation to cheat on a nuclear ban would be very great. In a world of no nuclear weapons, the nation that cheated and acquired or secreted just a few weapons would be the most powerful on earth. A secret or quasi-secret nuclear arms race could be reborn out of suspicion, and would be as dangerous as today's upward spiral. Moreover, since several other nations can or do possess nuclear weapons, a nuclear danger would persist even if the two superpowers scrapped their weapons. Abolitionists however argue that the very existence of nuclear weapons is a source of intolerable friction and rivalry. Therefore, the time has come to push past the interminable debate about "equivalence" and "stability" which are simply rationalizations for continuing to maintain nuclear arsenals.

It is relatively easy to formulate abolition proposals and plans since the conditions can simply be stipulated. The problem, however, is their political impracticality. A non-nuclear world clearly cannot be achieved unilaterally or wishfully. It can come about only through mutual agreement and action over time by all the nations possessing those weapons.

As we discuss elsewhere (see chapter VI), the committee does not support the concept of nuclear pacifism as U.S. policy, although we understand Christian pacifism as a personal option for those who for reasons of individual conscience embrace it. As an historic tradition, however, pacifism has not offered politically developed answers to the problems of modern tyranny, genocide, aggression and oppression. In the face of brutal international aggression, pacifism has generally offered only heroic individual responses, not a means of defending societies and nations.

There is, however, one developing concept that may merit further study. This is the concept of "civilian based defense."

This is a concept that is quite different from pacifism. It is an effort to find a "higher synthesis" of both just war and pacifism through the development and use of psychological, social, economic and political weapons to substitute for war. The principal proponent of this concept, Dr. Gene Sharp, argues that examples of effective non-violent sanctions (insurrection, civil disobedience, boycotts and strikes, mass demonstrations, etc) exist in history, and that we need to examine to what extent they can be applied to our present circumstances. The concept of "civilian-based defense" is an intriguing one. It does not, in our view however, apply to the current superpower conflict, nor is it at this stage an effective substitute for deterrence in the nuclear strategic sense — nor is it, in fact, so proclaimed by its proponents.[2]

The committee is drawn by the moral force behind the urge to abolish nuclear weapons. Indeed, as we describe elsewhere (see chapter VI) we believe a non-nuclear world should be our controlling vision. We need to hold such a vision, and to work toward interim moves that reduce reliance on nuclear weapons and lower the risk of nuclear war. If our imagination is filled with nothing but the thought of ultimate holocaust, then intellectual apathy and political paralysis may be the result. Hope is important. The committee recognizes, however, that complete abolition is a future hope and not a present possibility.

The Escape Into Usability

All nuclear weapons were at one time city-destroying bombs. Today, some experts argue, a wide range of nuclear devices exists, whose yield approximates that of some conventional bombs. Technological advances in precision, moreover, may soon create nuclear weapons with near perfect accuracy that could be aimed at military targets like tanks.

[2] Dr. Sharp is Director of the Program on Non-Violent Sanctions in Conflict and Defense at the Center for International Affairs, Harvard University. See his work, *National Security Through Civilian-Based Defense*, Association for Transarmament Studies, 1985. His most recent book is *Making Europe Unconquerable: The Potential of Civilian Based Deterrence and Defense*, Ballinger Books, 1986.

This line of argument seeks to suggest that the logic of mutual vulnerability can be nullified by making the vulnerability of societies appear limited. It argues that the scale and outcome of nuclear conflict can be controlled by the doctrine, strategy and types of weapons employed, that a limited nuclear war might be planned, fought and concluded more or less in accordance with traditional concepts and strategies of conventional warfare. To accept this argument means accepting several basic assumptions that we found open to serious challenge.

The notion that nuclear weapons are "usable" assumes that nuclear weapons are not fundamentally different from conventional weapons and can therefore be thought of and used in the same way. It is true that small nuclear weapons *can* be designed to have a blast yield below that of extremely powerful conventional weapons. But for what purpose? If one argues that nuclear weapons are usable because they can be made like conventional weapons in yield and accuracy, we ask, then why use nuclear force? Why not use conventional weapons? The natures of the two weapons are entirely different, and it is dangerous to blur the distinction between them. Conventional weapons have a known upper limit. The smallest nuclear weapons, however, stand at the bottom rung of an almost unlimited escalation ladder. Moreover, nuclear weapons generate radiation and other aftereffects which cause long-term genetic, biological and ecological damage. No nuclear device, however small, is free from this horror.

The argument that nuclear weapons are usable in war also rests on the central assumption that one side would hit only military targets, and that the destruction of life and property — referred to in the jargon as "collateral damage" — would be limited and therefore "tolerable." But this argument assumes that military targets are separate physically and geographically from non-military sites — which is not the case. "Military targets" include more than silos. If the purpose of using nuclear weapons is to destroy the enemy's military capacity, then "targets" must include air defense sites, radar sites, bases, ports, airfields, transportation networks, and the key industries that constitute the nation's war-making capacity. Clearly, the cities and populated areas of the United States and the Soviet Union are rich in "military targets." The implication that these are somehow separate things is a delusion. This means, in turn, that "collateral damage" associated with nuclear war-fighting strategies would be immense and terrible in absolute terms. Indeed, it might be indistinguishable from indiscriminate nuclear attacks on population centers.

The delusions inherent in "limited-use" scenarios become clearer when one considers what might happen if nuclear weapons were used in West Germany, a nation frequently cited as a possible opening battleground for the next war. Nuclear weapons would be set off in an area the size of Oregon, with a population twice that of the northeastern United States. As one of our witnesses put it, this would be like fighting a limited nuclear war through the Boston-Washington corridor at rush hour. Even an honest effort to strike only military targets would be impossible.

Proponents of limited or controlled use of nuclear weapons assume that the different levels of violence can be sealed off from each other, and that nuclear detonations will not be answered in an escalating spiral. They assume closed compartments of uses: a warning shot; a strike at a remote military site; a tactical battlefield detonation, and so forth. Such assumptions are hardly credible. A nuclear detonation at one level may be met by a nuclear response at the next level. It will be extremely difficult, in the chaos of war, to distinguish between uses of nuclear weapons. A targeting error, or an attack on tanks near populated areas, for example, would surely be misread and escalated. Under actual war conditions, a local commander — much less a national decision-maker — may not understand what enemy weapon was used for what purpose. The notion that there are dependable "firebreaks" between the categories of weapons or uses is unwarranted. In modern warfare the only meaningful firebreak is the one between conventional and nuclear weapons.

Designers of limited nuclear options argue that the flexibility of controlled, discriminate use would avoid mass destruction. It would create an alternative between surrender and suicide. This would give both sides a large stake in limited responses to avoid mutual destruction.[3] These theorists argue that large risks can be run, and that one side can climb far up the escalation ladder confident that nuclear violence will not spin out of control precisely because the cities remain vulnerable. The side that dominates escalation by inflicting more harm at each step, they argue, will be able to force the other to give in.

The committee could not understand why any of these assumptions would work. Why would gradual destruction of an enemy's military forces, in a limited nuclear war of attrition, give one side "victory" so long as the other side retained a counter-city strike capacity? Why would the other side choose to lose if it retained such an escalation capacity? Why, under such circumstances, would it be the Russians rather than the Americans who would make the concessions and stop?

The problems of command and control also deepen our skepticism about the feasibility of any kind of limited nuclear conflict. Control of nuclear war-fighting would require a smooth, responsive and flawless technical use of command, communications and intelligence functions. We found, instead, substantial doubt among experts that present command systems would be adequate to control nuclear exchanges.[4] Some, for example, pointed out that the command and control systems of the two superpowers are so tuned to each other that they could set off interlocking alerts, raising the possibility of a "feedback conflict': that is, one side sounds an alert, to which the other side reacts, causing the first side in turn to respond to an alert provoked by its own first alert. Even a nuclear alert could thus take on a momentum of its own, in much the way

[3] See, for example, Albert Wohlstetter, "Bishops, Statesmen and Other Strategists on the Bombing of Innocents," *Commentary*, June 1983, pp 15-35.

[4] See especially, Paul Bracken, *The Command and Control of Nuclear Weapons*. New Haven: Yale University Press, 1983.

that alerts acted like ratchets that propelled Europe into World War I.

Loss of command and control may also occur at several levels of attack. Some experts believe that "spoiling attacks" at a low level on command and control centers and systems could create communications disruptions and an unstoppable salvoing by local commanders. Up the escalation ladder, nuclear explosions themselves could disrupt communications between higher command centers, eliminating the control of nuclear forces.

The assertion that nuclear strikes can be controlled and limited is highly unreliable, for it fails to take into account how people react to violent conflict. Any decisions concerning what targets to hit with nuclear weapons will have to be made in haste, by harried political leaders in moments of deep strain and crisis. We know how difficult it is for governments to make decisions in any crisis involving the life and death of the nation. It is therefore irrational to assume that national leaders and their political advisors will make intelligent, careful decisions and choices under the unprecedented pressures caused by nuclear weapons exploding on their territory. There are few controls against escalation after nuclear weapons have been used. Any violence between great powers is inherently difficult to control, and it cannot be controlled unilaterally. Once nuclear weapons were used, there could be no assurance that the exchange could be stopped before terrible slaughter and destruction had occurred.

Beyond terrible slaughter and destruction lies an even more permanent horror: The whole range of lethal aftereffects of nuclear explosions — global radioactive fallout, the climatic changes of "nuclear winter," ozone destruction, fire-generated toxic chemicals, massive atmospheric chemical and particulate pollution, and long-term genetic, biological and ecological damage. In the past, experts in the nuclear weapons community concentrated on the *prompt* effects of nuclear explosions. However, recent investigation into the long-range aftereffects — about which we are still relatively ignorant — suggests forcefully that these would destroy or seriously threaten many forms of life. As two scientists recently wrote: "...we believe that the synergisms among the simultaneous occurrence of radioactive fallout, climatic changes, stratosphere ozone depletion and disruption of essential societal services could threaten more people worldwide than prompt nuclear effects."[5]

In our view the long range aftereffects and their consequences are too significant to ignore. If they are substantially true, nuclear weapons become their own deterrent. No nation could risk using any sizeable number of nuclear weapons against even an unarmed opponent without risking substantial self-destruction. To contemplate a preemptive strike would be to contemplate suicide.

In sum, we find no strategy for employing nuclear weapons that is rational. We see no useful military role for them. They cannot promise to end a war. They simply generate risk out of all proportion to any rational goal sought.

Escape Into Superiority

During the last decade, both sides have built nuclear arsenals far beyond the requirements of a retaliatory capability. This has been done despite the recognition of greatly redundant nuclear arsenals on both sides. Yet the call for more — and more effective — offensive weapons continues. On our side it is usually rationalized in one of two ways: (1) militarily, in terms of closing weapons "gaps" and "windows of vulnerability", or of countering specific Soviet strategic doctrines; and (2) psychologically and politically, as necessary to avoid the generalized perception that we are strategically inferior to the Soviet Union.

In a sense, these arguments reflect the continuing hopes and fears of the great powers: the hope of gaining advantages, the fear of suffering disadvantages. This dynamic, in turn, reflects a resistance to the fact of mutual vulnerability, and a corresponding compulsion to seek security unilaterally. Despite the reality of mutual vulnerability, there is an understandable

[5] Stanley Thompson and Stephen Schneider, correspondence and comment on nuclear winter, *Foreign Affairs*, Fall 1986, p. 177.

impulse to "do something." The result is a constant search for "edges" and advantage.

Many of the arguments for new and more offensive weapons are presented in military terms and in the context of "nuclear war-fighting" scenarios. Yet it seems to us that the proponents are really arguing that more weapons will enhance psychological and political perceptions of U.S. strength despite their questionable military advantage.

Such perceptions play an increasingly important role in policy making. In fact, it is clear to us that assessments of nuclear arsenals are made not on the basis of military considerations, but on how political leaders, experts, and the public judge the psychological impact of such arsenals — not just on ourselves and the Russians, but also on our allies and other nations. This leads to "playing games" by deliberately manipulating perceptions. Experts cleverly frame an argument by the selective choice of data that show their side to be "inferior" — and therefore in need of nuclear increment — while ignoring indicators that contradict this conclusion.

The game of "who's ahead" — with its constant comparison of numbers of weapons and its obsession with precise symmetries — is an attempt to escape from the reality of the nuclear world. It is a reversion to a pre-nuclear frame of reference in which tanks, battleships, and infantry divisions could by their numbers affect the outcome of a conventional war. But nuclear war is not conventional war. In old-fashioned warfare, a battle's outcome often could be rationally predicted by counting troop strengths or tanks or ships. But such a calculation has little, if any, relevance when both sides in a nuclear war can inflict cataclysmic damage in the space of a few minutes or hours, regardless of the number of weapons available to the opponent. What is important in a nuclear conflict is not the precise relationship of one side's missiles to the other's. Missiles do not fight missiles. What is relevant is the relationship of missiles to targets.

Another part of the search for marginal advantages is the argument that a successful surprise attack can be carried out with "tolerable" consequences. A most recent scenario sees a Soviet first strike using only a part of their land-based missiles to destroy most of our ICBMs, non-deployed bombers and submarines. The Soviets then threaten to hit American cities with a second strike unless we surrender.

We find such a scenario totally unconvincing. Why would the Soviets take such a monumental risk in the first place so long as the United States possesses a large, diverse retaliatory force, much of it secure at sea? The Russians, it seems to us, are not likely to act on the assumption that an American president would not respond to attack, but on their best estimate of how such a gamble might turn out for them. Why would the risks inherent in a first strike seem more attractive to the Russians than simply remaining at peace?

We consider it an illusion to believe that either side could claim to "prevail" in a nuclear war. The instantaneous destructiveness of nuclear weapons, and their lasting effects, make such claims meaningless.

We asked ourselves, for example, what would be the purpose of nuclear superiority, even if it were possible to achieve it. Surely, not to start a war. The purpose would be to intimidate, to press the other side to make political or territorial concessions that would improve the security of the "superior" power.

Two years ago Secretary Weinberger explained to a Senate committee: "If we can get a [defense] system which is effective and which we know can render their weapons impotent, we would be back in a situation we were in, for example, when we were the only nation with nuclear weapons."[6] The problem with this psychological/geopolitical blackmail theory is that it depends ultimately on a threat by the "superior" power to "go nuclear" if the other side does not yield to its demands.

The quest for nuclear superiority undermines the quest for nuclear security. If our goal is safety, we should want an

[6] Quoted in Gerard C. Smith, "Star Wars Is Still the Problem," *Arms Control Today*, March 1986, p 3.

arrangement of weapons that maximizes our ability to retaliate if the adversary strikes first, while minimizing the adversary's fear that we can destroy his retaliatory ability in a first strike. His confidence in his ability to retaliate after a first strike is central to *our* security; if he lacks confidence he may, in a crisis, have an incentive to go first.

We conclude, in sum, that we cannot escape from mutual vulnerability by building more and "better" weapons. Military "edges" have no meaning in these circumstances. Superiority cannot be acquired in the age of mutual nuclear abundance. Perpetuating conventional thinking can only lead us into deeper trouble.

The Escape Into Strategic Defense

In his speech to the nation on March 23, 1983, President Reagan called for a major effort to render nuclear weapons "impotent and obsolete" through the development of a reliable and total defense against nuclear ballistic missiles. With this concept — officially called the Strategic Defense Initiative (SDI), but known widely as "Star Wars" — the President launched the nation on a new course which seeks to replace the strategy of deterrence with a strategy of defense. In effect, he seeks an escape from the condition of mutual vulnerability by trying to construct a "thoroughly effective" protective umbrella over cities and people as well as over our nuclear forces.

The idea of "defense" is morally more comforting than the idea of relying on nuclear deterrence. Such phrases as "assured survival" and "it is better to save lives than avenge them" are appealing. It is natural and desirable to want to see our armed forces protect us by defending our national territory and people rather than by threatening the annihilation of other societies. The issue, however, is not whether defense is moral. It is whether a strategic defense is feasible, and whether pursuing it will lead to more security or to an extremely dangerous new arms race in space. What the President is saying, in effect, is that we can achieve a technological solution to the threat of nuclear destruction. The implicit promise is breathtaking:

We can protect ourselves without the need for arrangements with the Soviets; once the strategic defense system is in place, neither the Soviet Union nor any other potential adversary would ever again pose a nuclear threat to the United States or its allies.

In technical terms, the proposed layered defense system would take place in three phases: a "boost phase" — an attack on Soviet missiles during the brief (3 to 5 minute) period of liftoff from their silos; a "mid-course phase" — an attack on Soviet missiles during the 20 minute period when the warhead separates from the launcher; and a "terminal phase" — a final effort to destroy Soviet warheads in the last few minutes of their flight as they re-enter the atmosphere and begin falling toward their targets.

"Terminal defenses" could be built with existing technologies by firing projectiles or anti-ballistic missiles at incoming warheads. However, the weapons for "boost phase" and "mid-course phase" would essentially have to be space based, and are still early in the development stage. Moreover, even if scientific research were to achieve breakthroughs beyond what now seems likely, the practical engineering and operational problems necessary to deploy and coordinate a functioning system appear overwhelming. In addition, SDI would have to work effectively the first time it was used. No shakedown tests are conceivable in the kind of nuclear war environment for which it has to be designed. No system can meet such an unrealistic technical requirement. Also, given the extremely short "boost phase" of Soviet missiles, there would be no time for human response. The defense system would have to be activated by computers, removing the decision from human judgment and control. Leaving the issue of war or peace to computers is not a prospect we relish.

Aside from these staggering technological and operational difficulties, SDI is markedly susceptible to a wide range of Soviet counter-measures which promise to be far less expensive and less technically demanding to deploy than the defense systems themselves. Defense radars can be blinded, jammed or directly attacked. Enemy space mines can be positioned to trail kinetic kill vehicles in orbit and be detonated on command. Decoys can be used to confuse defenses. Mass attacks can saturate the defense. Dr. Richard DeLauer, former Under Secretary of Defense for Research and Engineering, said in 1983 that "with unconstrained proliferation [of Soviet missiles], no defense system will work." We concluded, therefore, that there is no possibility of building an effective full-scale defense system (an "Astrodome" defense in the current jargon) that has any prospect of protecting people and cities, especially if a determined adversary is simultaneously trying to find ways to defeat it.

Because the possibility of a near-perfect defense is widely dismissed, many supporters of SDI now argue in terms of lesser goals — partial defenses — as a means to reinforce deterrence and improve conditions for arms control. The proponents of SDI are thus splitting into different groups with quite different aims, and these must be carefully distinguished. One is the President's vision of a total defensive shield protecting all Americans and all American soil. The second concept, now emerging as the more prevalent view among official planners, aims at a partial defense system designed to protect missiles and strategic installations, not people and cities.

The partial defense argument goes as follows. First, because even partial defenses would greatly blunt the effectiveness of a Soviet ICBM attack, the Soviets would turn away from ICBMs as the centerpiece of their nuclear arsenal and would negotiate deep reductions in their number. Second, effective partial defenses that improve the survivability of the U.S. ICBMs would improve deterrence by reducing the incentives for a preemptive Soviet attack.

We do not find these arguments convincing. They fly in the face of most of the evidence before us, historical and technical. It is unrealistic to assume that the Soviets would ignore U.S. measures to neutralize the largest component of their nuclear retaliatory forces and thus remain passive in the face of U.S. efforts to alter the strategic balance to Soviet disadvantage. This is, in fact, the most dangerous implication of SDI: *it poses a direct threat to the present stability of the strategic balance.*

In December 1983 Secretary Weinberger asserted that an effective Soviet missile defense system "would be one of the most frightening prospects I could imagine."[7] Why? Because it would threaten to deprive the United States of its retaliatory capability and thus of the U.S. ability to deter a Soviet strike. Indeed, in a report delivered to the President on the eve of the November 1985 Geneva Summit, Secretary Weinberger wrote, "Even a *probable* [Soviet] territorial defense would require us to increase the number of our offensive forces and their ability to penetrate Soviet defenses to assure that our operational plans could be executed."[8]

Why should we expect the Soviets to respond differently to an American missile defense that challenges the effectiveness and reliability of their deterrent forces? The Soviets have repeatedly stated that their fear is precisely that the current SDI program, combined with continuing U.S. efforts to improve its strategic weaponry, add up to a U.S. attempt to disarm their Soviet deterrent. Thus both the United States and the Soviet Union agree that a defensive system in the hands of the other could pose an intolerable threat to which they would be forced to respond.

In arguing the case for SDI, President Reagan has stated that it would produce defensive weapons that only destroy the enemy's offensive weapons. But that is not the case. Some of the technology can also work for offensive purposes. In fact, space-based or space-oriented strategic weapons would be almost ideally suited to strike against targets in space or population centers on the ground below. It is important that the American people recognize the two-edged nature of the SDI sword, and that the Soviet's have a very real fear that the United States

[7] Quoted in Sidney Drell, "What's Happened to Arms Control?", Address delivered at the Conference on Nuclear Deterrence, University of Maryland, September 5, 1984.

[8] *New York Times,* November 18, 1985 Walter Pincus, "Weinberger Urges Buildup over Soviet 'Violations,'" p. A-20.

might develop component space defense technologies with offensive applications.

This Soviet reaction is something we must take seriously. After all, this is precisely how the United States reacted when faced with Soviet efforts to build a rudimentary defense system around Moscow in the late 1960's. The United States did not dismantle its ICBM's or seek to negotiate deep reductions in nuclear forces. Instead we increased the level of our offensive weaponry by developing multiple warheads (MIRV's) specifically to confuse and evade a Soviet defense system, should it be fully built. Such was the momentum of the program, moreover, that the United States proceeded to deploy the MIRV system even after reaching an agreement with the Soviets that neither side would deploy a serious ABM defense.

The United States, for its part, fears secret Russian progress in all strategic capabilities. President Reagan has publicly warned against, "loopholes that would leave the West naked to a massive and sudden Soviet buildup in offensive and defensive weapons." The Soviets fear our high technology. We, in turn, fear their secrecy and deception.

What all this underlines is the mutual nature of security in the nuclear age, and the peril of trying to achieve security unilaterally. The committee strongly believes that unilateral, unrestrained pursuit of SDI will foreclose efforts to significantly reduce strategic offensive nuclear forces. The Soviets have made clear that they will not agree to such reductions if they face unrestricted U.S. development of a defensive system. Thus, in the absence of an agreement to limit defense, an agreement on offense is neither militarily prudent nor politically possible. At the same time, without limits on offense, no effective defense is conceivable. If SDI is pursued and the Soviets react as predicted, the inevitable result will be a lethal arms race for the dominance of outer space.

It seems to us, therefore, that the question of strategic defenses — and specifically space based defenses — must be put on the negotiating table along with offensive weapons systems, and the interdependence of offensive and defensive systems must be reaffirmed.

At the Reykjavik summit, the United States insisted on the unlimited right to test and develop space-based anti-ballistic missile systems, while the Soviet Union maintained that work should not go beyond laboratory research. At the center of this disagreement stands the 1972 ABM Treaty. The Reagan administration has put forth a unilateral interpretation of the treaty, arguing that it permits testing and deployment of space-based weaponry. The great majority of U.S. experts, however, believe that the Reagan interpretation is wrong.

The Soviets claim, in effect, that the ABM Treaty bars the SDI program. The Reagan administration claims, in effect, that the treaty is irrelevant to SDI. Failure to resolve these differences threatens the principle of mutual security and invites unending increases in strategic offensive forces. In our view, the single most destabilizing consequence of the SDI is that it threatens to destroy the ABM Treaty.

Some administrative officials, notably Paul Nitze, insist that SDI is only a research program intended to provide an "evidentiary" base for deciding whether and how to proceed. Nitze has repeatedly made the point that defense technologies should be pursued only if they are survivable and cost effective at the margin, i.e., as cheap as systems designed to counter them.

However, the current SDI program seems clearly more than a research program. It has all the earmarks of a crash program intended to achieve a deployed system as soon as possible, without any pretense that it can be cost-effective and heedless of the Soviet reaction. Secretary of Defense Weinberger admitted as much in congressional testimony on January 12, 1987 when he endorsed early deployment of an "initial" network of missile defenses.[9]

Other Defense Department officials have begun to argue within the administration, and publicly, for early and partial

[9] *The New York Times*, January 13, 1987, "Weinberger Gives Strategy Outline on Missile Shield," p. 1.

deployment of some systems by the mid-1990's, even though they admit that the technology is not yet developed and that the cost would be well in excess of $100 billion. Moreover, the types of defense components under consideration for early deployment are of a kind highly vulnerable to counter-measures, and would require nonstop, costly improvements to stay effective. These new pronouncements advocate a course of action that would clearly violate the ABM Treaty and reverse President Reagan's offer at Reykjavik to forego deployment for ten years.[10]

Confusion and ambiguity thus characterize the SDI program. The President's dream of a total defensive shield, rendering nuclear weapons impotent, is utopian, far too nebulous to provide a basis for policy. On the other hand, the explanations and justifications of other administration officials indicate that their purpose for SDI is to enhance deterrence, not eliminate nuclear weapons. Indeed, the "deterrent enhancement" rationale has become the acceptable goal of SDI for most nuclear strategists. Thus after all its criticism of mutual assured destruction, the administration strategists end up advocating SDI in order to protect the American nuclear deterrent. Some in

[10] The defenses proposed for "initial deployment" apparently consist of sensors and orbiting battle stations capable of firing chemical rockets at incoming missiles, supplemented by ground-based anti-satellite weaponry. The rocket system needed to put aloft the space-based sensors and battle stations does not yet exist, however, and testing and deploying such weapons would violate the ABM Treaty. Doubts about the effectiveness of such initially deployed systems have been admitted by many of the proponents of early deployment themselves. Lt. Gen. Abrahamson, in a speech last December to the American Association for the Advancement of Science, said that the first partial defense capability would not provide perfect defense by any means, "and probably wouldn't act as a deterrent all by itself." The answer according to Abrahamson and his deputy, Louis Marquet, is to continuously improve the system by adding more and better battle stations and other weapons. At a congressional hearing in 1986 Gen. Abrahamson expressed the view that "there is no such thing as an ultimate weapon of any kind." When asked if what he foresaw were countermeasures and counter-countermeasures proceeding "in the area and sphere of strategic space defense in the same manner as we have seen elsewhere", Gen. Abrahamson replied, "Yes." See *Washington Post*, January 18, 1987, R. Jeffrey Smith, "Offensive Taken for Partial SDI Deployment," p. A-1.

the administration see SDI as a means to achieve military superiority, while others seek, through SDI, to push the Soviets into a more intensified arms race which they believe would drive the USSR into economic ruin.

Despite this conceptual incoherence, the program is developing a life of its own. Indeed, the danger is great that large appropriations for SDI for a number of years will create such vested interests in its continuance — jobs, military contracts, scientific research — that future Congresses and Presidents will face tremendous pressure to pursue the program, no matter how wasteful or unproductive the expenditures are. We foresee a steamroller effect, fueled by lobbyists, military contractors and technological optimists, creating such momentum that SDI could not be stopped no matter how obvious the danger involved in going forward. In fact, as we noted above, the push by Secretary Weinberger and others for "initial" SDI deployments is precisely an effort to nudge President Reagan toward a critical decision to move SDI from a research effort to a development/deployment program so that, as Attorney General Edward Meese has stated publicly, SDI cannot be "tampered with by future administrations."[11]

The committee unanimously concludes that SDI offers no prospect of achieving any of the visions that have given it momentum. We are extremely skeptical that it can ever create a shield to protect populations. It offers little prospect of substituting a defensive strategy for deterrence. And whether the stated aim is to shield populations or to enhance deterrence, the pursuit of SDI will inevitably trigger a dangerous new arms race in space, which will destabilize the nuclear balance. There are no technological fixes for our dilemma. A costly all-out competition to gain the "high-ground" of space offers absolutely no escape from the hard fact of mutual vulnerability.

---

[11] Quoted in *Washington Post*, January 18, 1987, "Offensive Taken for Partial SDI Deployment," p. A-1.

The Nature of Deterrence

We are left, then, with a continuing need for credible deterrence. How does one define deterrence? What is its function? What makes it credible?

The essence of deterrence is the probability of catastrophe if one side breaks the peace. Both the United States and the Soviet Union are vulnerable to nuclear attack, devastating retaliation, and a whole chain of ensuing consequences that neither side could control. Mutual assured destruction is not a strategy. It is a condition. That is, mutual assured destruction is the very likely consequence of any significant nuclear exchange between the two superpowers. The danger of mutual destruction, therefore, is not excised by elaborate strategies or doctrines. It exists in the very texture of the situation. It is an unavoidable consequence of nuclear war.

That each superpower is deterred is less the result of the other's explicit threat to inflict pain than it is, simply, the overwhelming general danger involved in starting a nuclear war. What matters most to U.S. and Soviet leaders is not who might win a localized conflict or a limited military action involving clients of the superpowers. What matters is the risk that such a clash might escalate to nuclear war. Mutual vulnerability breeds prudence, restraint, caution. It may not deter every hostile act in the competitive spectrum, but it does contain those that threaten the very survival of the would-be aggressor.

We want to stress this "existential" concept of deterrence, because much of the discomfort with and misunderstanding of the concept of deterrence is semantic. In most of the public debate, deterrence is treated as if it were a thing, an active agent. This is misleading. Deterrence is really a mode of analysis, a way to explain the relationship between nuclear weapons and political decision making. Weapons do not decide whether to be used or not; political leaders decide. If catastrophe is the probable consequence of using them, then rational political leaders will be deterred from doing so. The success or failure of deterrence depends on the quality of political judgment.

However, because nuclear weapons are the foundation of the deterrent effect, it is common, as Theodore Draper has pointed out, "to transfer the hatefulness of those weapons to the balance that inhibits their use." To reject deterrence because we recoil from the nature of the weapons on which it is based is to give up one of the few — perhaps the only convincing rationale why the weapons cannot be used for any sane, credible purpose. " … It is the link with politics that is the best hope of deterring the employment of nuclear weapons."[12]

More than three years have passed since Draper wrote that passage, and many developments, Reykjavik not the least among them, have underlined the importance of the "link with politics" as a vital component of deterrence.

Deterrence is in fact a word of broad meaning, for other factors normally combine with military strength to make a potential aggressor decide against war. Arms control agreements are themselves a part of the structure that governs such crucial decisions.

The effectiveness of mutual deterrence is thus not based on elaborate strategies of punishment or denial. It is based on the fact of nuclear impasse. The superpowers are at a standoff.

Their most valuable pieces on the chess board are subject to check; their nuclear weapons must be held back, for if they are used everything valuable will be destroyed. Because neither side is suicidal, they carry on their competition by maneuvering indirectly on the periphery. We believe the nuclear standoff is a source of stability, for deterrence is not based on a fragile balance. Deterrence has, in effect, two sides. One side is the appreciation that terrible things will happen to the nation that takes any action to violate the nuclear impasse. The other side is the implication that terrible things will *not* happen if one refrains, that restraint by one side will be rewarded with restraint by the other. The point is crucial. It means that the general state of U.S.-Soviet relations bears directly on the

<hr />

[12] Theodore Draper, "Nuclear Temptations," *The New York Review of Books*, January 19, 1984, p 43.

prospects for war or peace, that the perception of each other's goals and intentions is as relevant as military doctrine or strategy.

Deterrence can be undermined by self-delusion. Leaders who attempt to escape the logic of mutual vulnerability run the risk of talking themselves into believing that nuclear weapons can, in fact, be used, that nuclear war can be controlled and limited, when in truth these options are unrealistic.

To acknowledge the condition of mutual vulnerability is not to argue that it is a satisfactory state of affairs or a preferential choice (although it is certainly preferable to instability). Nor is it to argue that deterrence has no other form or scale than that which exists today. But mutual vulnerability and deterrence are basic conditions with which we must come to terms. Moreover, we must understand that the primary way — perhaps the only way — out of dependence on the current balance of terror is through a steady modification and improvement of political relationships rather than through technological fixes.

In conclusion, we see no feasible escape from the fact of mutual vulnerability. Nuclear weapons can neither be disinvented nor made useful. Superiority cannot be attained, nor can an impenetrable defense for the American people and their allies be built in any foreseeable time frame. Wisdom, it seems to us, is not to be found in theories, scenarios or arguments that seek to evade the overwhelming central fact of the nuclear revolution. Wisdom lies, instead, in recognizing mutual vulnerability as a compelling truth, and in working to make the nuclear impasse more stable and less dangerous. Only when the nuclear stalemate is accepted as the prevailing reality, and "deterrence" is understood as the existential condition that it is, can we move with reasonable confidence toward arms reduction and reduced dependence on nuclear weapons.

Chapter IV
THE U.S.-SOVIET RELATIONSHIP

The conflict between the United States and the Soviet Union has dominated international relations since the end of World War II. It has polarized Europe into competing alliances. It has also been a central factor shaping the attitudes and policies of Japan, China, India and other nations. It has converted much of the developing world into either spheres of East-West influence or arenas of competition.

This conflict comes from major differences in the international goals of the two nations, in the interests which they pursue, and the values in which they believe. It is easy to misunderstand this rivalry. Some people see it in demonic, Armageddon-like terms. Others dismiss it as simply the result of misunderstandings or ill-will, easily dissipated. Yet the differences between the two nations are indeed deep, as one expert on Soviet affairs has summed up:

> We are divided not only by our different interests as great powers but also, and more importantly, by diverse values and beliefs to which we subscribe, by different historical experience, and by devotion to different systems and rules of behavior which are based on different principles and priorities of human existence, human values and political beliefs. To understand each other is not easy, and it is also not enough...Understanding each other as far as it is possible does not end the problem but leads only to its re-emergence on the rational level.[1]

[1] Seweryn Bialer, "The Psychology of U.S.-Soviet Relations." Extended version of the Gabriel Silver Memorial Lecture, School of International and Public Affairs, Columbia University, April 14, 1983, p. 26

The development of nuclear weapons has limited the way that this rivalry can be resolved. As the last chapter detailed, once each superpower acquired a second-strike capability and effective nuclear parity—as is now the case—the strategic relationship between them became one of mutual vulnerability, and, therefore, of strategic stalemate. Mutual vulnerability has handcuffed the United States and the Soviet Union to one another, and has placed severe limits on the way they can confront and struggle with each other. Indeed, the recognition of this fact by both sides has probably prevented the competition between them from deteriorating into war; under old, "conventional" circumstances, war might have occurred before now. Therefore, we can assume that a central goal of each nation is to avoid nuclear conflict.

Survival, then, clearly depends on mutual restraint and cooperation. While mutual vulnerability requires them to avoid direct confrontation, the underlying rivalry forces their competition into indirect channels: to Third World or regional conflicts, to the use of surrogates, the maintenance of alliances, to constant maneuvers for some putative psychological or political advantage.

Each side is tempted to seek political advantage by exploiting the other's desire to avoid war. Tension centers around judgments about "resolve," and results in the generalized attitude that one nation needs to demonstrate its willingness to risk war as a sign of "strength."

The danger, of course, is miscalculation that could lead to war. Fortunately, leaders on both sides have been extremely cautious; indeed, they have been far more cautious than abstract reasoning about strategy would have suggested. The caution springs from their sense of general danger. Mutual vulnerability has in fact bred prudence and restraint in the leadership of both sides, irrespective of declared policies or theories of conflict.

And yet both sides continue to arm. The prevailing American view is that we cannot trust the Russians. The prevailing Soviet view is that they cannot trust the Americans. Each tends to see the actions of the other as illegitimate, and to view the relationship as a struggle. The American tendency to apply moral judgments of "good" and "evil" to this competition increases U.S. rigidity and stimulates the belief that "hardnosed" responses to Russian actions are required. Many Americans believe that if the Russians favor something we must oppose it, and if they oppose something we must favor it. Russians, no doubt, take the same stance. This situation, in turn, feeds insecurities on both sides. The United States and the Soviet Union are more prepared to trust the arms race as the protector of their unilateral security, than to trust agreements with each other.

We find considerable hope, however, in recent actions that indicate these basic attitudes may be changing on the Soviet side. The evidence is growing that new Soviet leadership has made a judgment that nuclear weapons cannot be used to gain or preserve any valued political goal, and therefore that Lenin's doctrine of a final clash between capitalism and communism has been rendered inoperative by weapons technology. In his major five hour speech to the 27th Communist Party Congress in February 1986, Gorbachev summed up as follows: 'This means realizing that in the present situation there is no alternative to cooperation and interaction between all countries. Thus the *objective* considerations have taken shape in which confrontation between capitalism and socialism can proceed only and exclusively in forms of peaceful competition and peaceful contest." From this have flowed his efforts to stabilize the U.S.-Soviet relationship, to deal seriously on a range of important security issues, and especially to reach an arms control agreement that will halt the gathering arms race in space.

The committee has concluded that a determined effort on both sides must be made if progress is to be achieved. In the next few pages we concentrate on what Americans can do because this is something over which all of us can exercise some control. We recognize that this has to be matched by similar efforts from the Soviet side. For Americans to move toward breaking the cycle of antagonism and suspicion requires, we believe, at least three steps. First, reaching a greater self-awareness of the mainsprings of our own national attitudes and behavior. Second, achieving a balanced understanding of Soviet psychology, purposes, policies, and methods. Third, identifying the elements of a program of cooperation that would be bold enough to stimulate and sustain constructive efforts on both sides, yet practical enough to serve as a blueprint for workable, day-to-day improvements in U.S.-Soviet relations. The premise must be joint recognition of common security. It is to these matters that our report now turns.

Looking at Ourselves

Perhaps the first task for Americans is to look introspectively at ourselves. President John F. Kennedy, in his famous speech at American University in April, 1963, calling for a limited test-ban treaty, said: 'Americans are neither omnipotent nor omniscient." He warned that "we must not see a distorted and desperate view of the other side; we must not see conflict as inevitable, accommodation as impossible, and communication as nothing more than an exchange of threats." In the harsh climate of current U.S.-Soviet relations, this is a warning worth repeating, and one we disregard at our peril.

It is a well-known axiom that people instinctively identify their nation-state with good — even with the deity — while assigning evil to other nations. Our national survival today depends on transcending that common pitfall. But doing so will require substantial changes in our habits of thought and attitudes toward the external world in general, and the Soviet Union in particular.

This will not be easy. How citizens of any nation perceive and act on the external world is largely determined by historical experience, and their own national values. The historic and formative experience of the United States has made it difficult for Americans to deal with other nations as equals. While Americans continue to evolve toward an egalitarian society at home, their encounters with the rest of the world have been of a different character. America's heritage of separation—both physical and philosophical—helps explain this discrepancy. The early settlers were exiles or refugees from societies where social and religious conflict and class barriers ran deep. Indeed they fled from persecution and sought personal freedom in conditions of cooperation, accord, and consensus.

What is unique in American history is the *absence* of permanent contradictions among our notions of society's basic ends and purposes. As a nation, we are therefore impatient with and intolerant of basic conflicts of ends. We have little experience in the kinds of ideological and social conflict that are imbedded in the national life of many nations.

This heritage has shaped our attitudes about political conflict, relations with other nations, and the use of power. The committee sees at least four significant consequences of this legacy.

First, because the American experience has been relatively successful, Americans are tempted to believe that the values that spring from this experience have universal application. Yet in fact, much of our political stability and economic success have depended on special conditions and circumstances almost unique in modern history. This, in turn, has produced a sense of exasperation with conflicts that endure, like those in the Middle East, or between India and Pakistan, or Greece and Turkey.

Second, Americans tend to consider cooperation and concord as "normal." We think of foes or countries with different views and objectives in disparaging terms because hostility and conflict are, by definition, abnormal. This attitude affects the way we think about negotiations with adversaries. We resist the notion of negotiating with someone we regard as an enemy, partly because we suspect that a compromise with someone who holds different principles means that our own principles may somehow be corrupted, and partly because we do not want to legitimize a foe. We resist a middle ground, and insist on negotiating "from strength," so that we can dominate the proceedings and assure a favorable outcome. We doubt that foes can be trusted to keep agreements, or to negotiate openly

69

and fairly. Because Americans are accustomed to negotiating domestically within a framework of fundamental consensus on ends and principles which are taken for granted, we tend to assume that negotiating with the Russians or another foreign adversary ought somehow to be like the bargaining between the steelworkers and U.S. Steel Corporation.

The United States also has difficulties dealing with friends. Our political tradition and preference is for unilateral action and preserving our freedom of maneuver. We resist arrangements or policies we cannot control, and we are reluctant to allow others to share in the determination of our policies. Historically, we have vacillated between withdrawing from the world and involving ourselves totally in order to manage it.

Third, from our historical experience and tradition of individualism comes a particular kind of pragmatism in politics and problem solving. Americans seem to think about policy responses to complicated issues in terms of simple mechanical, technical or organizational formulas. There is also a natural optimism, a pride in being a "can-do" society.

While a case can be made for optimism and self-confidence, we must recognize the limits of a technical, pragmatic, "engineering" approach to complex political issues. For this creates the temptation to look at the instruments of policy as policy itself, to confuse the tools with the objectives. It can lead to the conviction that American ingenuity and technology can somehow solve any issue if we just work at it hard enough. The "Star Wars" initiative strikes us as a good example of our exaggerated confidence in technology.

Our heritage and tradition, and the values and beliefs that flow from them, have created ambivalences that perhaps we have not recognized. There is, for example, an ambivalence in the "image" we want to present to the world. We frequently stress our revolutionary beginnings, and our "new world/new nation" character. Yet we also stress our support for order, stability, legality, and peaceful nonviolent change — which is close to the posture of a status quo nation. There is ambivalence in what one authority has called "the two languages we speak" the language of power and the language of harmony and consensus.[2] On the one hand, we extol the virtue of our power, might, and strength. We "stand tall." Yet we also praise harmony, community, consultation and working together, international law, and unselfish motives. There is in the American ethos "a tension between an instinct for the use of force and a drive for harmony."[3]

In foreign affairs this ambivalence is troublesome. To advance our interests, we sometimes use force: direct military intervention, covert action, military assistance, and we tend to believe our use of force is somehow redeemed by our good intentions. By relying on the assumption that others surely understand that our intentions are good, we feed our propensity to misunderstand the reactions of other nations. We often fail to realize that other nations judge us as we judge them: by actions and not by intentions. We often fail to understand that other nations see behind our acts the presence of our overwhelming power. A common American view holds that the United States can be trusted, but others cannot. Americans project a sense of moral superiority in the use of power. The committee believes these ambivalences are neither cynical imposture nor hypocrisy. In our view, they are honest polarities, but we must be more aware of them and their implications for the conduct of foreign policy.

The United States must find a more stable basis for coexistence and cooperation with the Soviet Union. It must be a mutual undertaking based on mutual recognition of the necessity to coexist. It takes two to cooperate, and cooperation by the Soviets will depend on their perception that the United States is a vigorous, effective, and vigilant competitor. But the American people and our government must also accept the fact of interdependence in the matter of survival. Our continued resistance to this reality is one measure of the changes required in our attitude and outlook if we are to contribute to an improvement in U.S.-Soviet relations.

[2] Stanley Hoffmann, *op. cit.*, p. 181.
[3] *Ibid.* p. 181.

Looking at the Soviets

It is never easy to understand another nation. So much gets in the way. It is particularly difficult in the case of the United States and the Soviet Union. For however alien or unacceptable the beliefs of the Soviet leaders may seem to us, we should remember that our beliefs look the same way to them. It is as difficult for them to understand us, as it is for us to understand them.

We do not wish to imply that the conflict between the two nations is simply one of misunderstanding or misperception. As we have repeatedly noted, the substantive differences between us are sharp, and the conflict will not be simply wished away. On the other hand, it is essential that we understand each other as well as we can, so that we may avoid misperceptions, illusions and errors that confuse and distort U.S.-Soviet relations.

American beliefs and views about the Soviets range along a spectrum. At one end is the "evil empire" belief: that the Soviet leaders are bent on world domination by conquest and revolution; that their hostility to us is unremitting, and that we have no significant interests in common. At the other end of this spectrum is the notion that differences between the United States and the Soviet Union are the result of basic misunderstandings, and that, at heart, the American and Russian people are very much like one another. The policies people advocate for dealing with the USSR vary depending upon where they are located along this spectrum of beliefs. We have identified four distinctive policy approaches currently advocated by Americans.[4]

- Those who see the Russians as implacably dedicated to world domination. In this view, the United States can only commit itself to "winning" the ideological and power struggle.

[4] *These conclusions are drawn largely from Voter Options on Nuclear Arms Policy, 1984*: A Briefing Book for the 1984 Elections; Daniel Yankelovich, Robert Kingston, Gerald Garvey, eds., published by the Public Agenda Foundation and the Center for Foreign Policy Development, Brown University.

Therefore, the United States needs to achieve military, technical, and economic superiority, and must be prepared to meet and overcome any Soviet challenge. Tensions with the Soviets can be reduced only by surrendering to them.

- Those who see the relationship as constantly and sharply competitive, but one that can also be "managed" in the familiar balance-of-power pattern. This view does not include the belief that either superpower can eliminate the other, or that the relationship can be transformed into a grand "social contact" or peaceful condominium. Rather it calls for an eternally vigilant coexistence and a constant balancing of military, economic, and political forces.
- Those who see the possibility of converting the "management" of the rivalry into a network of practical negotiations and concrete understandings on specific matters, especially arms control. Over time, with patience, the rules of the game can be broadened, leading eventually to a more stable and constructive, if not entirely harmonious, relationship.
- Those who hold the view that the concept of "winning" is deleterious and will become progressively more dangerous. They seek peaceful actions to reverse the psychology of hostility. If the U.S. acts in a conciliatory and reassuring way, this view holds, the Soviets will respond with equal reasonableness. If we can reverse the psychology of enmity, nonhostile and non-competitive relations might result. In this view, major improvement in U.S.-Soviet relations could lead to a fundamental restructuring of the international order.

Soviet Realities

The central point on which these different concepts vary is the degree to which one believes that the hostility of the Soviets can be overcome, managed, controlled or diminished, and by what means. In studying carefully the range of expert opinion available to us, both written and oral, we reached agreement on a number of major points we believe are supported by evidence and reason. We present them here as an effort to place Soviet realities in perspective.

First, the Soviet Union is an outgrowth of a Russian state which has lived for centuries on the borders of Europe. It now extends across Asia, peopled by a complex and growing patchwork of ethnic groups. It has been dominated by European-oriented leadership, and has in this century participated, to a certain extent, in the development of modern Europe, including the creation and elaboration of the European state system. But it is also an Asian power, with interests and concerns in that region of the world, especially in terms of China and Japan. Moreover, there are 130 languages spoken in the Soviet Union, and across its 11 time zones there are more than 100 significant ethnic groups; Russians, in fact, constitute a minority. It may well be this characteristic, more than any other, that shapes the Soviet Union of the next century. For example, by 1990, one-third of the Soviet armed forces will be Moslem non-Russians. Despite this heterogeneous character, however, the Soviet government continues to find ultimate support in the nationalism and patriotism of all the Soviet people.

The Soviet economy may be inefficient, backward, and hobbled by over-centralization. But it is also large and able to resist outside pressure. Despite weaknesses, the Soviet Union is a strong, operating society with great underlying staying power, both political and economic. Its leaders and people are determined and able to resist outside pressure. The committee found few who would maintain that the Soviet Union is in an internal destructive crisis which, if the United States pressed hard enough, would lead either to its demise or to a loss of national will.

Second, the Soviet regime is a communist dictatorship given to arbitrary and brutal methods of rule both at home and where its influence reaches abroad. However, although expansionist in their aim, the Soviets do not believe offensive war is the way to achieve their goals. Their central struggle — and fear — centers on the defense of their internal system, their national boundaries, and their buffer zones. They aim at military power sufficient to hold "imperialist" (that is, in the Soviet view, American) power in check, while permitting socio-economic forces (which include Soviet support for "wars of national liberation") to determine the future. They pursue large military programs to reinforce their superpower status, and to ensure that they maintain their side of the strategic balance. They have accumulated nuclear war-fighting capabilities, which generate anxieties in the West about Soviet objectives. However, it is logical to assume that Soviet military programs reflect, at least in part, their own concerns over the size and pace of U.S. military build-up and the superiority of U.S. technology.

Third, the ruling hierarchy has become a large bureaucracy with a strong vested interest in the perpetuation of its power and privileges. The Communist system has become oligarchical. The party is in no danger of internal subversion or external overthrow. Yet it wages a relentless and even ruthless war on dissent. Americans are unavoidably repelled by this ugly characteristic of the Soviet regime. But we also need to understand that this internal repression is rooted not in a doctrinaire fanaticism or in cynicism, but in the obsession with discipline and control over its people. The notion that many Americans have that Soviet leaders are either fanatics or cynics is a misleading caricature. (Indeed, if they were purely fanatics their policies would be less cautious and far more risky. If they were pure cynics, the richer western nations would find it much easier to seduce them into a comfortable collaboration.) The nature of Soviet leadership is more complex than this. Moreover, there is now some evidence the reform efforts of the new leadership under Gorbachev are aimed at reducing the rigidity of the Soviet system, at providing more room for diversity and creativity, in order to render Soviet society more productive and efficient.

Fourth, Soviet leaders calibrate their interests not much differently from European or American politicians. Like all politicians, they try to reconcile beliefs and values with the exigencies of given situations and problems and to be both successful and effective. They deal with gaps between beliefs and reality by employing all of the same psychological devices of rationalization as their counterparts elsewhere.

Fifth, the Soviet Union remains a highly bureaucratic, conservative state that finds it extraordinarily difficult to manage change. Belief in the tenets of Marxism-Leninism, in the words of one authority, "has long ago burned out in the Soviet leadership stratum."[5] Whatever Marxist-Leninist doctrine may say about a classless society, Soviet leaders have created an oligarchic and highly-stratified social-economic internal status quo which they defend with great vigor. At the same time, we are now witnessing the concerted efforts of a new generation of Soviet leadership to reorganize and neutralize the system against public inertia and entrenched bureaucratic self-interest.

Sixth, if the USSR has become a conservative, status quo regime at home, it nevertheless retains a revolutionary attitude toward the existing international order. It continues to seek expansion of its influence and power in the world, particularly in the Third World.

Soviet leaders apparently see no contradiction between following a conservative, status quo policy at home, and pursuing an active foreign policy that aims at disintegrative change abroad. Both are, in a sense, rooted in the same source: a basic insecurity and obsession with preserving the "home base" against nations and groups that seem to threaten it.

But ironically, this basic insecurity has produced a Soviet foreign policy whose tactics, strategy and approach have generally been pragmatic, gradual, and often cautious. Soviet foreign policy, while seeking change, has been characterized by a strong resistance to high-risk ventures. (The attempt to place missiles in Cuba in 1962 appears in retrospect to have been an aberration, and one which contributed directly to the downfall of Premier Nikita Khrushchev.)

We find no evidence that this has changed. Soviet leaders hold a general expectation that history is on their side, and that in the long run things will work out in their favor. (Americans, of course, feel the same way about their system.) But in the

[5] Bialer, *op. cit.*, p. 24. See also Dimitri Simes, "The New Soviet Challenge," *Foreign Policy*, Summer, 1984, pp. 113-131.

concrete formulation of short-range and middle-range Soviet foreign policy, USSR leaders conduct themselves much as leaders of other nation-states. Their foreign policy stresses what is prudent and possible, evaluates both temptations and opportunities, and carefully considers dangers and obstacles. The aim of maximizing Soviet influence is thus carried out within the bounds of prudence.

Seventh, the notion that Soviet foreign policy derives from a "master plan" for world domination and operates on a secret timetable, is without support, even though some Americans believe this.

Finally, there is nevertheless a contrast between the way the Soviets and the United States approach foreign policy issues and negotiations. Peace and co-existence do not carry the same meaning in the East and the West. To the Soviets, they are strategies for continuing the struggle to achieve their goals. To the Americans, they imply equilibrium, "live and let live," and an end to conflict. These differences of approach lend themselves to exploitation by the Soviets in a way that puts a special premium on U.S. persistence, patience, and consistency.

Misperceptions

Prevalent American misperceptions about the Soviet Union seem to us to constitute both difficult obstacles to a genuine understanding and serious pitfalls for policy formation.

We have already referred to the error of underestimating the Soviet Union's stability and staying power under harsh conditions, its economic strength, and its ability and determination to resist outside pressure. Yet there remains a prevalent belief in the United States that this nation (or the West) can exercise significant leverage over internal Soviet affairs. Some Americans also believe that the Soviet system is in such decay that unremitting pressure will bring down the political structure, or that pushing the Russians into a more intense arms race will bankrupt their economy. Others believe that a relentless "push and shove" policy will erode the will and power of the Soviet leadership to resist external pressure.

We do not minimize the weaknesses and problems in the Soviet system. Internal collapse or change is not entirely inconceivable. But it is not at all evident that the United States (or the West) can affect change within the Soviet system, let alone rapid change. Indeed, the instruments of western coercion do not look very impressive, given the political and economic realities in the United States and Europe. The successful resistance of NATO allies to U.S. pressure to prevent their participation in building a Soviet-Europe gas pipeline and the successful pressure by American farmers for continuing grain sales to the USSR offer recent examples of the difficulty.

A more sophisticated version of this argument states that one can affect and change Soviet policy by exerting influence on internal Russian structures, because the source and formation of foreign policy have their roots in the domestic system. Dr. Richard Pipes, for example, has written that change in Soviet foreign policy behavior:

> . . .will come about only from failures, instabilities, and fear of collapse and not from growing confidence and a sense of security . . . attempts to restrain Soviet aggressiveness by a mixture of punishments and rewards fail in their purpose because they address the symptoms of the problem, namely aggression, rather than the cause, which is a political and economic system that induces aggressive behavior. The West, therefore, should in its own interest encourage anti-Stalinist forces and processes active inside the Soviet bloc. Such a policy calls not for subverting communism but for letting communism subvert itself.[6]

While we believe that the United States has the power to frustrate Russian ambitions that are threatening to us, we do not agree that the United States has the power to manipulate internal Soviet affairs, or that American pressure can reorient

[6] Richard Pipes, "Can the Soviet Union Reform?" *Foreign Affairs*, Fall, 1984, pp. 56 and 61.

Soviet policy-making away from international ambitions. One can hope that internal change will occur, and over time something like that might happen. But it is folly for Americans to believe that we have the power to bring about internal Soviet change, and thus to base a whole U.S. strategy on such a fantasy.

There is also a misguided tendency in this country to dehumanize and demonize the Soviet leaders, to disparage the nationalism of the Soviet people, to deny their fear of war and to accuse them of callous indifference to the casualties of war. To think and speak of them as ideological automatons programmed for world domination, as some Americans do, poisons the atmosphere and increases the risk of angry, irrational responses by the Kremlin leadership. This makes achieving a minimum of mutual trust and forebearance more difficult than it need be. Worse, by encouraging the American people to think of the Russian people as "communist" abstractions, lacking both the normal imperfections and redeeming qualities of humankind elsewhere, this attitude takes a step toward the idea that destroying them would be desirable. At best this will cause us to make serious foreign policy mistakes. At worst, in a crisis, such irrational thinking could lead to war.

We are disturbed by the common American belief that what is good for the Russians is bad for us, and vice versa. There may be some items in the relationship that fit that formula, but survival and coexistence are not among them. To conceive of everything this way is to condemn us both to disaster. As we have mentioned, there are some cherished goals — peace, survival — which can only be gained or lost together. This zero-sum perception, of course, is a reflection of the underlying distrust and suspicion that we have referred to, and that has led both nations to what may be the single greatest obstacle: the belief that each can provide for its own security without help from the other.

Finally, we note that a body of opinion in this country considers it a grave error to believe that the two superpowers are "morally equivalent." There are, to be sure, qualitative moral and ethical differences between the Soviet and American systems and the set of values and goals each subsumes. What disturbs and alarms us is the extent to which this proposition has developed into a self-righteous moralizing about the "good" Americans and the "evil" Soviets. In some educational, civic and official circles this has become an absolutist view which appropriates moral superiority to the United States, but denies any legitimacy to the Soviet Union as a state or as a great power with broad interests. This view also rejects all arguments that the Soviets have any grounds to distrust us or to feel aggrieved. It considers the notion of parity with the Soviets — politically, militarily and economically — to be impermissible.

Several things are wrong and dangerous with this mind-set:

— Prudentially, it poisons the atmosphere and undermines the "live and let live" forbearance on which the avoidance of nuclear war depends.

— Ethically, it is pharisaical. It leads to self-congratulation that blinds us to our own defects and shortcomings. It tempts us to pass the kind of definitive moral judgment on others which, in our religious tradition, it is not in our province to do: "Judge not, that ye be not judged." (Matthew 7:1)

— For Christians such a mind-set cannot adequately be reconciled with the tenets of their faith. While Soviet behavior may in many cases merit the adjective, "reprehensible," or even "evil," a Christian can never lose sight of the fact that the Soviet people and their leaders are human beings created in the image and likeness of God; that Christ died for us all, the just and the unjust; and that we are all sisters and brothers at the foot of the cross.

Where All This Leads.
We have focused in this chapter on what Americans need to bear in mind if they are to move into a process of mutual accommodation. However, improving the relationship between the superpowers is a two-way street. The Soviet approach to the U.S.-Soviet conflict is at least as harmful and counterproductive as erroneous American attitudes and misperceptions. The

Soviet leaders' paranoid secretiveness, dismissal of Western concerns and principles, self-righteousness as agents of a worldwide historical process, and view of other nations' policies as a vast conspiracy, are all examples of their contributions to misunderstanding and confrontation.

We should, in response, subscribe publicly to the principle of the interdependence of United States and Soviet security, the permanence of the nuclear stalemate, the mutual suicide of nuclear weapons use, and the imperative of coexistence.

We need to understand that we can defend ourselves and our values without developing an "enemy mentality'; that truculence and belligerence are not to be mistaken for strength and firmness; that reaching out to reconcile neither corrupts nor betrays our own ideals and principles.

We need to acquire a realistic understanding of the Soviet nation. This means, in our minds, much more than just a knowledge of the history, culture and language of the Russians and other peoples of the Soviet Union. It should also include an awareness that the Soviet Union's people embrace some 55 million Christians—Orthodox, Catholics, Lutherans, Baptists and members of many other Christian churches and sects. In addition, we need to develop as deep and accurate an understanding as we can of Soviet thoughts and feelings about us. This kind of understanding can be clinical and objective. As one authority put it, "If we do not clearly recognize their [Soviet] hostility to us, we will not be tough in the ways we should be tough, and if we do not clearly recognize the ways in which they are human beings...we will not be reasonable and cooperative in the ways we must be in order to survive."[7]

In practical terms, all this might translate into:

— regular meetings between American and Soviet political and military leaders;

— regular meetings between American and Soviet religious leaders;

[7] Ralph K. White, *Fearful Warriors: A Psychological Profile of U.S.-Soviet Relations.* New York: The Free Press, 1984, pp 9-10.

— wider and more intensive university programs in Soviet studies;

— more extensive U.S.-Soviet contacts and exchanges, both official and unofficial. We see no dangers in this, and much to be gained, in counteracting an isolated and defensive mentality in the USSR.

We need to accord to the USSR a recognition of its status as a world power, and to accept the legitimacy of its 275 million human beings as an enduring functioning society. This has nothing to do with moral judgment or "moral equivalence." It is a historical fact. Nothing may be harder for American officials and citizens to do than to recognize this need, and to halt the condescension and even contempt we sometimes demonstrate toward the Soviet Union. Yet few other things would do more to break the reciprocating cycle of antagonism and distrust. This is an initiative we should undertake not because we believe it will be automatically reciprocated, but because it is simply realistic, and accords with the facts.

If the American people can achieve a more balanced perception of the Soviet Union, we believe a better basis will exist for working to strengthen coexistence and mutual survival. Such improvements will not resolve the basic conflict of purposes and values between the two dominant nation-states. Each in its own way is a messianic power committed to extending its particular political philosophy in the world. Even if we arrive at a political relationship that greatly strengthens the chances for avoiding nuclear war, both Americans and Soviets are likely to continue to live with a range of fundamental differences and in a state of continuing competition, even as we strive to enlarge the areas of mutual interest.

But improvements in relationships and accommodations can bring the conflict between us to a more rational level, even if they cannot dissolve it. Greater understanding and a mutual self awareness will also strip away the worst distorting myths and emotional fears. In time, a more trusting relationship may be established by a long and gradual process, in which every step contributes to the next.

The members of the committee are under no illusion that any of this will be easy, or that the task of reconciliation will be devoid of tension, or even crisis. But neither do we see grounds for despair or for concluding fatalistically that the future cannot be different from the past. The American Catholic bishops' pastoral encapsulated the point eloquently:

To believe we are condemned in the future only to what has been the past of U.S.-Soviet relations is to underestimate both our human potential for creative diplomacy and God's action in our midst which can open the way to changes we could barely imagine.[8]

---

[8] *The Challenge of Peace: God's Promise and Our Response.* Pastoral letter of the U.S. Catholic Bishops on War and Peace. Text as published by *Origins*, N.C. Documentary Service, May 19, 1983, Vol 13, No. 1, p 24.

Chapter V
NEGOTIATION
OR CONFRONTATION:
THE ARMS CONTROL AGENDA

The committee has concluded that agreements to control and reduce nuclear arsenals are central to a stable relationship between the two superpowers, and, therefore, to their mutual security. As a consequence, we believe that the political path of seeking arms control agreements is the only realistic and safe route to reduced dependence on nuclear weapons — and, eventually, to a non-nuclear world. Unfettered competition in weapons and military technology cannot make either superpower more secure; they can only increase the risks of war. The alternative to an effective arms control regime, in our view, is an ever more destabilizing and dangerous race in both offensive and defensive weapons.

This is all the more important now because recent changes in Soviet leadership, and the views currently presented by Mikhail Gorbachev (see chapter IV), present us with the best opportunity to conclude effective arms control agreements since the early 1960's. Such an opportunity, however, may be transient. If we squander it, we will have irreversibly worsened the world's nuclear dilemma. That is a legacy we should not leave our children.

In this chapter we seek to summarize the elements that seem to us essential to an effective arms control policy, and provide our recommendations in this regard.

Criteria for Success:
Equivalence, Reductions, Stability and Verifiability

Debates among experts over negotiating objectives, nuclear weapons programs and arms control agreements have become extraordinarily complex and difficult to understand. Facts and figures can be marshaled to prove a positive or a negative case for almost any agreement or weapons program. Acronyms and obscure terms reinforce the expertise of the debaters, but limit comprehension by those outside the debate. When expertise becomes a source of obfuscation rather than enlightenment the average citizen must rely on common sense in seeking to understand the broader essentials of the problem. We have concluded that there are four standards by which agreements, as well as new nuclear weapons programs, should be judged by citizens as they struggle with their civic and moral responsibilities. These criteria are equivalence, reductions, stability and verifiability.

First, *equivalence*. Agreements must, over time, provide for overall equivalence in nuclear forces between the United States and the Soviet Union. Agreements cannot be sustained if there exists a great disparity between U.S. and Soviet nuclear forces. Attempts by either side to achieve superiority are provocative, dangerous, and ultimately futile.

The committee has concluded that overall equivalence now exists between U.S. and Soviet nuclear forces, despite the fact that each side has chosen to accumulate its forces in a different way (see table I). The Soviets, for example, are deeply wedded to land-based missiles. In contrast, the United States has chosen to divide its forces into three more or less balanced parts — the "triad" of land-based missiles, sea-based missiles and bomber forces.

TABLE 1
STRATEGIC BALANCE AS OF JANUARY 1, 1987[1]

U.S. Warheads / Launchers			USSR Warheads / Launchers	
2202	1014	Land-based ICBM	6420	1398
5632	640	Sea-based SLMB	3344	928
3538	278	Bombers	940	160
11374	**1932**	**Totals**	**10704**	**2486**

[1] *Source:* Arms Control Association staff from data supplied by the Department of Defense, the Joint Chiefs of Staff, and the Arms Control and Disarmament Agency.

Because of these differences in force structure, attempts to reach agreements based on precise numerical equality in specific categories of weapons will invite failure in negotiations. American presidents have gotten around this problem in the past by aggregating different kinds of forces, with each side free to chose different ways to reach equal aggregate limits. For example, the SALT II agreement allowed both sides to have equal aggregates of land and sea-based missiles carrying more than one warhead, although it did not demand equal numbers in each category.

Some experts argue that agreements of this kind are really unequal in favor of the Soviet Union because the Kremlin's land-based missiles are larger than American land based missiles. These experts are concerned about the disparity in missile "throw-weight" (the payload that missiles can carry) which, in their view, mocks argeements based on numerical equality in delivery vehicles or warheads. They point out that Soviet missiles, being far larger than ours, can carry greater numbers of warheads; that is, the Soviets could use their superior thrust power to add more warheads to their present delivery vehicles in violation of agreements.

We find this argument a clear example of how debates among experts can distort common sense. The U.S. and the Soviet Union have between them approximately 50,000 nuclear weapons of all kinds. Heated disputes over the Soviet advantage in missile throw-weight have meaning only in scenarios of a protracted nuclear war, which assumes many thousands of detonations. We believe such nuclear war-fighting scenarios have little bearing on reality, as both sides are likely to be destroyed in the first few hours of a nuclear war, and with the use of only a small percentage of the available weapons.

A second basic criterion for genuine nuclear arms control is *reductions*, for at present high levels of weapons, equivalence alone is not an adequate measure of stability. High levels of weapons create the perception of a threatening nuclear warfighting capability. Thus, Soviet and American leaders need to demonstrate their commitment to controlling armaments by reducing them. Future arms control agreements must provide for equal forces that ratchet down the nuclear arms competition. Reductions also symbolize the political commitment by both sides to make the world a safer place.

A third basic criterion for the future must be *stability*. Given the human potential for rationalization, any nuclear weapons system can be said to contribute to deterrence and thus to stability. But the easiest way to distinguish fact from fallacy is to listen carefully to one side's concerns about the other side's forces. For stability is achieved through mutually acceptable trade-offs that reduce or eliminate those forces on each side that the other finds most threatening. Weapons (like the MX) that are both highly threatening and vulnerable to attack provide the least stability, for in moments of crisis, political leaders might be tempted to use such weapons or risk losing them. Equivalence and reductions must accordingly be related to the consideration of stability, so that both sides feel secure with the strategic balance as the level of weapons progressively declines.

The basis for equitable trade-offs that lead to a more stable balance of forces appears clear from the stated concerns of both sides. For many years, American officials have been concerned by the large number of Soviet land-based missiles carrying multiple warheads. For its part, the Kremlin is deeply disturbed by the Reagan administration's Strategic Defense Initiative and the new highly accurate submarine launched intercontinental missile (D5). Without agreed trade-offs involving reductions in these offensive forces and strict controls on defensive forces, the objective of stability cannot be reached.

The fourth criterion for judging the value of an arms control agreement is *verifiability*. At the outset of our inquiry, we saw verification largely as a technical issue. Now we see it primarily as a political issue. Questions of verification boil down to a matter of weighing conflicting risks. Every arms control agreement poses some risks, including the risk that the Soviet Union will not abide by its provisions. But there are also risks in not reaching agreements.

Given the existing nuclear weapons capabilities on both sides, the risks associated with verification do not loom large, in our view, compared to the risks of an intensified and unregulated arms competition on earth and in space. Moreover, to gain any meaningful advantage by violating an agreement, the Soviets would have to make an effort so large that the U.S. would surely detect it and have time to take countermeasures.

Verification and Compliance

Verification and compliance questions are intrinsically important. When the United States enters into an agreement with the Soviet Union or anyone else, it should expect the terms of that agreement to be observed, and it should possess the means to monitor its observance. Negotiated agreements without adequate verification do not inspire public confidence.

We realized from our discussions with expert witnesses that determining what constitutes "adequate" verification is not easy. But we are much impressed by U.S. "national technical means" of verification — photo reconnaissance satellites, radars and other devices — which enable the United States to monitor Soviet military activities. These technical devices are very effective, and can be supplemented by cooperative agreements that help each side keep track of the other's forces. Still, some risks must be accepted in order to reach agreement.

A specific example of these risks relates to negotiations over a comprehensive test ban to bar all nuclear weapons tests. In 1963, President Kennedy and Premier Khrushchev were deadlocked over the question of detecting underground nuclear tests. At very low levels, these tests could be muffled and were sometimes difficult to distinguish from earthquakes. For these reasons, President Kennedy and Premier Khrushchev agreed that some number of inspections would be required to assure mutual compliance with a total ban on testing. For President Kennedy, at least seven annual inspections in each country were necessary, for Premier Khrushchev, only three. Owing to the political pressures on each side, neither leader felt he could compromise further, so the opportunity for a comprehensive ban was lost. Instead, they signed a Limited Test Ban Treaty that barred testing in the atmosphere, under water and in space, where detonations were relatively easy to detect without on-site inspection.

Even so, the Limited Test Ban Treaty was criticized by those who argued that above-ground tests, conducted in deep space or behind the moon, could not be detected by U.S. monitoring capabilities. The Kennedy administration did not contest this point, but argued that such tests would be difficult to carry out and would not, in any event, provide the Soviet Union with substantive military capabilities. This general distinction between the conceivable and the plausible strikes us as a useful one in dealing with questions of compliance.

During the time of these negotiations, the levels of radioactive substances in children's teeth and in mothers' milk caused by atmospheric nuclear tests were on the rise. It was neither rational nor moral to reject a ban on atmospheric tests because we could not fully monitor Soviet compliance in deep space or behind the moon. Our children who were growing up then, and their children today, are healthier because of this treaty.

From this case study, and others we have investigated, we have drawn a useful lesson: It will always be possible to cheat under the terms of an arms control agreement, but we must not be so attuned to the risks of cheating that we forego important agreements that will increase our security.

Approximately eight hundred (800) underground nuclear tests have taken place since the Limited Test Ban Treaty was signed and each side has continued to deploy more advanced nuclear forces. In retrospect, the failure of President Kennedy and Premier Khrushchev to compromise their differences and achieve a comprehensive test ban agreement is a tragedy of major proportions. Such an agreement could have effectively halted the development and deployment of all new nuclear weapons since 1963.

Just as it is impossible to devise an agreement immune from cheating, it is also impossible to devise an agreement that clearly spells out every single obligation of the parties. Over the lifetime of an agreement, new developments will arise that were not anticipated at the time of signing. Advances in technology may not be adequately foreseen in treaty texts, and each side may choose to define its obligations in different ways. An agreement may also contain deliberately ambiguous provisions, where neither side was able to accept precise language or to forego particular military options for the future. For all of these reasons, compliance questions are bound to arise after an agreement has been signed.

Because so much is at stake in compliance controversies, we believe it is wise *not* to rush to judgment when evidence of a compliance problem comes to light. Cheating may have occurred, but the trouble may also be the result of ambiguities in treaty language, administrative mistakes, or any number of other possible explanations. When a compliance problem arises, it makes sense for the United States to work quietly through diplomatic channels to gain a clearer picture of the facts, and to seek diplomatic solutions that maintain the viability of arms control agreements that are in the interest of both sides to observe.

We note with great apprehension that unresolved compliance problems have begun to mount since 1979. Virtually all of them relate to differences in interpretation or to grey areas in treaty provisions. One Soviet compliance problem seems clear-cut, however: the Soviet Union has constructed a large radar in Siberia, instead of on the Soviet periphery as required by the ABM Treaty. The Soviet Union has also complained about U.S. compliance with arms control agreements. Most Soviet complaints appear to be marginal, but cannot be dismissed out of hand. For example, early warning radars currently under construction in Greenland and the United Kingdom are far from the periphery of the United States, as required by the ABM Treaty. The U.S. explanation is that these are not new, but simply "modernized" facilities — but if the superpower roles were reversed here, U.S. officials would no doubt cite these facilities as violations. The committee is convinced that compliance issues — like verification problems — are primarily political in nature. They can be overcome if both sides see their interest in preserving existing agreements. The private forum created by the SALT agreements to handle compliance questions — the Standing Consultative

Commission (SCC) — worked effectively during the Nixon, Ford, and Carter administrations. There is no intrinsic reason why it cannot continue to do so. But the Reagan administration has ceased to use it as a forum for resolving differences. Instead, it employs the SCC merely to issue citations of Soviet "violations," a practice the Soviets have now begun to reciprocate. Compliance problems are bound to be more intractable during a period when U.S.-Soviet political relations are strained and each side questions the other's intentions toward existing agreements. Without a political relationship between the two countries that promotes compromise and reaffirmation of existing agreements, the agreements will unravel[2].

The "Framework" Concept

An effective agreement on offensive forces requires limitations on all nuclear weapons systems with ranges over 600 miles. These forces are quite diverse, including long range cruise missiles, SS-20s, Pershing II's, intercontinental land-based and submarine-launched ballistic missiles, and "heavy" bombers. Despite the wide variety of these weapon systems, it is possible to limit deployments so as to allow each side to have equal aggregates of various types of forces. Presidents Nixon, Ford and Carter used this approach, recognizing that each side would choose different ways to arrive at equal limits. Within this framework, both sides would be able to reduce their offensive forces by agreement at regular intervals. The SALT I accords provided

[2] The allegation that the Soviets have continually violated key arms treaties has been seriously challenged by many U.S. experts. A report issued by Stanford University's Center for International Security and Arms Control in mid-February 1987 concluded that "overall U.S. and Soviet compliance with the terms of existing arms control agreements has been good. . . . A recent perception that compliance has been poor is false." This perception, the report concludes, was "created" by the Reagan administration's deliberate search and exaggeration of the military significance of alleged Soviet violations. The group issuing the report was a distinguished group of arms control experts and former officials. They included Sidney Graybeal and Robert Buccheim, former U.S. commissioners on the Standing Consultative Committee, Soviet scholars Alexander Dallin and David Holloway, physicists Sidney Drell, Wolfgain Panofsky and Leo Sartori, and William Perry, former Under-secretary of Defense for Research and Engineering.

one such framework. The SALT II Treaty provided another, more complete, basis for agreed reductions in the major categories of strategic forces.

But the superpowers cannot make much progress in negotiations if they regularly attempt to impose new frameworks or to resolve every conceivable strategic concern and every detail at the outset. The immediate need is to establish a framework to control nuclear forces and to provide a basis for reductions. The "framework" concept is, in our view, the most practical procedure for making progress and maintaining negotiating momentum. Agreement on a framework need not await the "fine print" necessary for follow-on agreements. Subsequent reductions and specific rules and conditions can be hammered out more easily if the framework has been agreed to. In short, it seems clear to us that with a concerted effort actively supported by both heads of state, a framework which limits deployment of nuclear forces can be erected.

At the Reykjavik summit President Reagan and General Secretary Gorbachev came close to agreement on just such a framework. The two sides were in basic agreement on an overall ceiling of 6,000 strategic warheads and 1,600 strategic launchers, with Gorbachev proposing "counting rules" for bomber forces agreeable to the Reagan administration. On intermediate-range missiles, Gorbachev accepted the U.S. proposal for "zero" U.S. and Soviet missiles in Europe, and a limit of 100 Soviet warheads in Asia and of 100 American warheads in the United States (a concession which Secretary of State Shultz termed "breathtaking"). Gorbachev also agreed "in principle" to U.S. principles for verification of such an agreement.

In the committee's view this framework would provide an agreement that would be in the strategic interest of both sides, and would constitute the first truly meaningful reductions in the arms race since nuclear weapons were invented.

The Reagan administration has offered proposals that would cut heavily into Soviet forces in both START and INF negotiations. In INF, the Soviets have basically accepted the "zero option," which is the administration's position, because it conforms with the Kremlin's priority of removing the U.S. nuclear forces from Europe. In START the Soviets have been far less flexible, predicating deep cuts on strict controls over SDI. At Geneva, the U.S. has sought to ban mobile ICBM's, a weapon we had previously sought to promote. At the same time, Washington has announced plans to proceed with two mobile ICBM's. Assertions that arms control agreements injure American security have no merit, in our judgment. Would the United States be better off today if both superpowers had continued to poison the atmosphere with repeated tests of nuclear weapons — a practice stopped by the Limited Test Ban Treaty? Would the United States be safer if both superpowers continued to excavate new silos for multiple warhead missiles — a practice barred by both the SALT I and II agreements? Would the United States be better off it both superpowers had deployed costly anti-ballistic missile defenses during the last two decades — a practice barred by the ABM Treaty?

Nevertheless, we clearly face the serious problem of securing public and congressional support for agreements *after* they are negotiated. The last three nuclear arms control agreements — the Threshold Test Ban Treaty signed by President Nixon in 1974, the Peaceful Nuclear Explosions Treaty signed by President Ford in 1976, and the SALT II Treaty signed by President Carter in 1979 — have never been ratified by the United States. American domestic politics is thus revealed as a central problem. The President can reach arms control agreements with the Soviet Union, but the record indicates a serious lack of national political consensus to ratify these agreements and regard each as one more link in a long chain that strengthens our security. No single agreement will solve all our problems. The key to success, as several of our witnesses told us, is to sustain a long-term process resulting in a series of mutually reinforcing strategic arms control agreements.

The committee believes that our controlling vision should be the elimination of all nuclear weapons, but we recognize this is not an attainable goal in the foreseeable future. The immediate, practical requirement is to establish an agreed negotiating framework and to proceed with proposals for balanced, stabilizing reductions of nuclear forces. The committee believes the urgent need now is to emphasize the downward direction, rather than the ultimate goal. In this sense, we should heed the advice of Freeman Dyson in his book, *Weapons and Hope*:

> Revolutions are risky and should not be undertaken without careful preparation. . . Disarmament seems impossible for the foreseeable future, despite the powerful arguments based on Christian principles that nuclear weapons and other weapons of modern warfare constitute idolatry and will lead to holocaust. Over a long period of time substantial disarmament may indeed be feasible in connection with basic changes in world governance. The concept should be made a serious long-term goal, rather than dismissed as hopeless ideology.[3]

The Strategic Defense Initiative

At this point, the most significant obstacle to an arms control framework agreement and to deep reductions in strategic nuclear forces is the U.S. insistence on an unfettered right unilaterally to develop and deploy space-based defensive systems. The Soviets have said that they will not agree to reductions in offensive strategic weapons if we pursue the unrestricted development of SDI. The United States, for its part, has so far refused to link the two.

In chapter III we evaluated SDI at some length, but it would be useful to repeat here our key judgments:

• Unrestrained pursuit of SDI will foreclose the opportunity to reach agreement on reductions in strategic offensive forces. No agreement on offense is possible without an agreement on defense; and without limits on offense, no effective defensive system is possible. Any transition to a "defensive strategy" without control over offensive deployments would be extremely unstable.

[3] Freeman Dyson, *Weapons and Hope*, New York: Harper and Row, 1984, p. 12.

- Deployment of defensive systems by either side without comparable simultaneous deployment by the other would be dangerously destabilizing. SDI cannot unilaterally substitute a defensive strategy for the deterrent effect of mutual vulnerability.
- SDI offers virtually no prospect of ever becoming a magic shield for protecting populations and rendering nuclear weapons obsolete. Technological uncertainties, exorbitant costs, and Soviet countermeasures all make it unrealistic to hold out the prospect of an "escape" from mutual vulnerability via a unilateral technological "fix."

As we noted in chapter III, the Reagan administration's reinterpretation of the ABM Treaty to permit unfettered testing and development of defense technologies based on "exotic" physical principles is inconsistent with the letter and the intent of the treaty, as well as with the understanding of both countries as demonstrated by their actions over the past thirteen years. Such a unilateral interpretation would erode the treaty to the point of collapse and destroy that document's main goal — crisis stability. One of the principal purposes of the treaty was to avoid sudden "break-outs," i.e., to insure considerable "lead-time" between the moment when it might become apparent that one nation had decided to build a territorial missile defense and the point at which it could deploy one. The new interpretation would permit virtually any development and testing of space-based directed energy devices and sophisticated space or air-based sensors, and would thus eliminate the treaty's assurance of significant lead time before a deployment could take place.

Secretary Weinberger and some other U.S. officials are urging an early partial deployment of space weapons, but there is clearly division within the administration as to the feasibility or desirability of such a deployment. Both the Secretary of State and the Chairman of the Joint Chiefs have indicated that insufficient information is available to decide on early deployment, and most experts have argued that it would be imprudent in the extreme to begin a partial deployment with no idea of what the ultimate system "architecture" is to be. Furthermore, early deployment of the type of weapons talked about — kinetic kill weapons — would be prohibited under *either* the traditional or the broad interpretation of the ABM Treaty. Thus advocacy of early deployment would appear to be attempting deliberately to scuttle the ABM Treaty.

Secretary of State Shultz has publicly described the criteria that he believes should apply to SDI programs[4]. To be deployed, he has said, space-based defensive systems must be "technically feasible," "survivable" and "cost effective at the margin" — the criteria earlier announced by Paul Nitze. The Secretary has added two additional criteria, however. No phased deployment should begin until there is a clear understanding of how this would be developed into a full-scale defensive system; and, secondly, no deployments should be made unless they contribute to crisis stability. These seem to us to be reasonable criteria and guides for proceeding with SDI. However, they are not consistent with the administration's new interpretation of ABM, nor, of course, with Secretary Weinberger's proposals for an early partial deployment of an SDI system.

How then should the United States proceed? The committee believes that we should proceed at a measured pace with a careful research program into defense technologies both as insurance against "breakouts" and to determine the potential for such technologies. Work on SDI, however, should be in conformity with the intent and purpose of the ABM Treaty, i.e., it should make clear the division between laboratory research and development on the one hand and engineering development and "field testing" on the other. We should at the same time, however, seek to work out with the Soviet Union specific agreements on the application of the ABM treaty terms to SDI-related research.

We also believe that we should seek with all deliberate speed to work out a "package" covering agreement on reasonable limitations on SDI in return for the deep reductions in strategic offen-

---

[4] The Secretary's remarks were made on the David Brinkley television program, and reportedly had been approved by the President. A summary of his remarks was contained in the *Washington Post*, February 14, "President Requests List of Possible SDI Tests," p. A4.

sive forces outlined in the framework discussed at Reykjavik. The task would be not to simply stipulate a number of years for guaranteed ABM Treaty adherence, but rather to define adherence, i.e., reach agreement on how the treaty provisions might be applied to SDI — and to Soviet space research — in a manner acceptable to both sides.

The argument that accepting limitations on SDI will "kill" the program is unwarranted. The choice is not between going ahead full speed on SDI or killing it, but rather how to regulate an SDI research program consistent with an arms control regime based on the ABM Treaty.

Anti-satellite Weapons

In the near term, the contest to capture the high ground of space is symbolized by the testing of weapons to destroy satellites in low earth orbits. The Soviets have a crude anti-satellite capability, which they have offered to dismantle under an "ASAT" agreement. The United States is beginning to test a far more advanced and versatile anti-satellite weapon system. The Reagan administration has resisted an agreement banning ASAT flight tests citing concerns over verification and the need to destroy Soviet satellites in the event of war. If either side proceeds to fully test and deploy advanced anti-satellite weapons, the other will surely follow. Both will thereby feel more insecure, for each will possess the means to disable the other's "eyes" and "ears" — a condition that could greatly increase the dangers of miscalculation and thus of accidental war. We see no end to the generation of new military requirements and threats that will follow if ASAT's are deployed. Therefore, the committee believes that an agreement banning all testing and deployment of anti-satellite weapon systems is urgently needed.

The risks associated with verifying compliance with an ASAT test ban agreement appear to the committee to be minimal compared to its considerable benefits. In any event, each side would retain some residual capability to damage the other's satellites — for example, by using existing ballistic missiles that could be re-programmed to detonate in space. Therefore, although a perfect agreement for ruling out all means of destroying satellites cannot be devised, it does not follow that we should forego a useful, stabilizing ASAT ban simply because it is less than perfect. Arms control opponents certainly do not expect perfect performance when they consider the purchase of new weapon systems.

Political Accountability for Progress in Arms Control

The committee believes that our elected officials have a moral obligation, and thus a political responsibility, to reach arms control agreements with the Soviet Union that make this world a safer place. Our elected officials are the repository of the public trust. They have a responsibility to promote the general welfare and to work for the common good. There are many serious threats to the things we cherish, but none is so compelling as the threat of a nuclear war. The burdens of public office impose upon our elected officials a responsibility to reduce the likelihood of nuclear war, reduce nuclear arsenals, lessen tensions between nations that possess nuclear weapons, and prevent others from acquiring them.

We feel strongly that when officials stand for election to high public office, they must be held accountable for their performance in upholding this most essential of all public trusts. Individual citizens can and must inform themselves about these issues, and they have a responsibility to demand progress on the control of nuclear arms. For until the American people consistently demand success in arms control from our elected officials, success will continue to elude us.

Accountability should not be a partisan political matter. We believe that the electorate should hold all persons elected to national public office under the same rules of accountability, regardless of party affiliation. Nuclear arms control is not a matter of party politics, but a national and moral imperative.

For those who already serve in positions of public trust, the judgments of the electorate should be made on the basis of their deeds while in office, rather than their words. Have new agreements been negotiated during the incumbent's terms in office?

Has he or she voted to approve or disapprove prudent arms control measures? We categorically reject the view that an endless build-up in U.S. nuclear weapons capabilities somehow serves to preserve, protect and defend the Constitution, whereas nuclear arms control agreements do not.

Some may argue it is unfair to insist that American political leaders succeed at this difficult task of nuclear arms control, since Soviet leaders are under no comparable pressure from their electorate. What would prevent Soviet leaders from sitting on their hands and letting time work in their favor?

We have several responses to these concerns. As we see it, time is now working against both sides in the arms race. Every year that passes without new agreements adds more refined and threatening offensive nuclear capabilities to the equation, leaving both sides less secure.

There are solid reasons to believe that it is in the Soviet Union's own self-interest to negotiate a framework agreement expeditiously and to follow up with periodic percentage reductions. Current Soviet attitudes on arms control are more forthcoming than they have ever been, and the opportunity for significant and reasonable arms control agreements is better than at any time since the 1960's. General Secretary Gorbachev clearly understands, far better than his predecessors, the need for a condition of genuine mutual security, in which neither superpower lives in fear of attack from the other.

As we have stressed repeatedly, controls over opposing nuclear weapons capabilities — both offensive and defensive — provide the only reliable basis for mutual security, and the entire history of the nuclear arms race demonstrates that insecurity breeds an intensified competition. For prudential, political and moral reasons, our political leaders have no choice but to pursue nuclear arms control with all diligence.

Conclusions

The considerations outlined in the preceding pages reflect the Committee of Inquiry's strongly considered view that we stand at a decisive juncture in superpower relations. Either we recognize the centrality of mutual security and the consequent need to move further down the road of arms control agreements, or we witness the collapse of our efforts and the deadly acceleration of nuclear competition into space. Neither the unilateral accumulation of nuclear arsenals and technologies, nor technological fixes, nor nuclear war-fighting strategies can defend that which we hold dear. U.S. defense policy must be reoriented away from the simple reliance on weapons accumulations, and must recognize the mutuality of security in this nuclear age. It is our firm conviction that agreements to control and reduce our nuclear arsenals are central to the mutual security of the United States and the Soviet Union. We believe we should move urgently toward an overall "framework" agreement which would cover both reasonable limitations on the search for defensive technologies and deep reductions in strategic offensive forces along the lines of the "Reykjavik framework." We should not miss the opportunity now before us to achieve the most dramatic progress in the history of U.S.-Soviet arms control.

The committee also wishes to stress the possibility of forward movement along the whole spectrum of nuclear arms issues:

- The United States should agree to halt nuclear weapons testing underground as a concrete step toward negotiating a long overdue comprehensive test ban (CTB). The Soviet Union has four times extended a unilateral moratorium on nuclear testing, inviting us to follow suit. We have so far refused and have continued testing, and the Soviet's have now resumed their own testing. A CTB is, in our view, essential to halt the development of new and more threatening weapons and to inhibit the acquisition of weapons by other countries.
- The United States should agree to continue its moratorium on the testing of ASAT weapons against targets in space so long as the USSR exercises similar restraint.
- The United States should gradually reduce the flight testing of ICBM's and SLBM's. Such a halt would be an effective means of halting new weapons development.

- The United States should begin to destroy obsolete tactical nuclear weapons under appropriate safeguards and invite international observers to witness the destruction.
- The United States should begin planning now for a series of follow-on agreements within the "Reykjavik framework" such as were envisioned as follow-on reductions from the SALT II ceilings.

A ten percent annual reduction from Reykjavik totals over five years, for example, would bring weapons on both sides down to about 3,000 strategic warheads (plus other nuclear weapons). But it would be a drastic improvement over the present situation of excessive inventories, and would permit the two nations to consider additional steps toward true disarmament on the eve of the twenty-first century.

Chapter VI
MORALITY, RELIGION AND THE NUCLEAR DILEMMA

As the preceding chapters have detailed, decisions about nuclear weapons, nuclear strategy, and superpower relations raise the most urgent moral questions of our time. One of the basic goals of this study has been to lift to a conscious, explicit level the moral dimension of the choices before us, and to recognize the consequences and implications for these political and security choices of our religious beliefs. This is an elusive goal. The application of traditional moral doctrine on warfare from earlier Christian thought is inadequate for the nuclear age. We are in a vastly different situation from our Christian forebears. The moral and ethical implications of nuclear weapons constitute a profoundly different challenge.

Religion, Ethics and the Use of Armed Force

In the effort to determine the moral validity of a position or policy, ethicists raise four questions to provide guidance. The mature ethic must involve all four fields of inquiry in every instance:

Goals. What are the goals or ends? What values does one want to achieve? Ideally, these will be peace, justice and freedom for society as a whole, as well as for individuals. Are these motives guided by selfish interest at the expense of others or does good will for all parties and the wellbeing of the whole provide our motive?

Motives. Why does one want to achieve these particular goals? What are the motives and intentions? Are these motives guided by selfish interest at the expense of others or does good

103

will for all parties and the wellbeing of the whole provide our motive?

Means. How shall one achieve one's particular values? What is the relationship of means and ends? How much do the latter justify the former?

Consequences. Where will the decision lead? Will other values be achieved or destroyed on account of this action? By taking a given course, one eliminates the possibility of doing something else. What would have been the probable consequence of following the alternative?

In addition, competing moral claims present unique dilemmas. There is, for example, the problem of present versus the future — how much risk may we inflict on future generations, for example, to protect our freedoms in this generation? But, equally, is survival so absolute that we have the right to forego risks to preserve access to the values we cherish for future generations? As regards allocation of resources: How much can we spend on defense, itself a legitimate concern, when social needs, poverty and disease require resources? There is also the global vs regional consideration: To what extent do we have the right, in coping with world issues, to impose problems on other nations or peoples? And there is the question of "lesser evils" in our efforts to balance the claims of these four ethical considerations.

Obviously, an act or policy is easy to judge when good goals, good means, and good intentions bring good consequences without sacrificing moral claims. The dilemmas arise when good intentions bring bad consequences; or when good consequences cannot be achieved without causing other consequences which sacrifice other important claims; or when good ends are sought by bad means. The maintenance of a deterrent force, for example, is usually posed as one in which imperfect means are used to seek what one hopes is a good end, with the result that it creates paradoxical problems of competing claims and values.

What a Christian posits as goals, motives, appropriate means and acceptable consequences are determined, shaped and judged by the Person and Gospel of Jesus Christ. We encounter Christ through the Holy Spirit especially in worship and at prayer. We come to understand more fully who He is by studying the Bible and the theological traditions which we have received. It is the biblical vision of the world — as one created and sustained by God, scarred by sin, and redeemed in Christ — that helps us understand human nature, realize the stubbornness of sin, know the meaning of forgiveness, respond to God's reconciling love, and dare to extend that love to friend and adversary alike. It is understanding Jesus' nature and love for humanity that informs, nurtures and compels us to make a commitment to peace-making both in personal relations and public affairs.

At the heart of the perennial debate about the role of the church and religion in political and secular affairs rest humankind's recurring questions about the relationship between moral principle and political judgment. How can the tenets of Christian faith be applied when decisions are based on collective requirements and responsibilities? How much, and to what degree, does religious faith mandate choices of strategy and tactics or determine interpretation of events?

In the area of politics and morality there are two extremes. First, one's personal beliefs may oppose, or place restrictions on, political behavior aimed at defending the national interest as defined by its leaders. Thus, one may try to rationalize moral principle, to deny its "political" applications, or to argue that religious principles apply only to individual conduct and not to the "real world" of international affairs and foreign policy.

Second, at the other extreme is the temptation to react wishfully and emotionally, to sentimentalize. The former Archbishop of Canterbury, William Temple, once noted that the Christian response to wrongs is too often to "bleat fatuously about love." Faith and theology do not of themselves suggest practical political policies. Without the knowledge and understanding of practical evidence about the contemporary world, as one of our witnesses has written, church declarations lack credibility[1].

[1] Shinn, *op. cit.*, p. 373.

A moral principle can undoubtedly be implemented by a variety of valid alternatives. Unquestionably, the practice of national and international affairs requires judgment and choices that are utilitarian and "political." Yet the biblical tradition in which we stand will not allow us to say that morality and public policy are somehow separate things. Faith and theology compellingly establish the foundations of political choice. Tactical choices whose import and consequence go against Christian moral principle cannot be justified. Faith may well require rejection of certain lines of reasoning and bar certain actions when we see the conclusions and results to which they lead.

Christian witness therefore is more than just individual moral rectitude. It requires a forthright proclamation of religious values and their relevance to the political, social and economic conditions that shape our lives. The traditional preacher's message of "be good and do good" is an incomplete summation of God's call to us. Our faith requires us to exercise a commitment which addresses not only personal sin, but also the systemic ills of institutions and governments — "to speak truth to power" as the prophet Nathan did to King David.

During the entire history of the church, Christians have struggled to reconcile the ethics of Christian love with the use of armed force. In the very eary days of the church, when Christians had no political responsibility and when most believed that the Second Coming was imminent, it was relatively easy to accept a pacifism which said that since killing was wrong, all war was always morally wrong. The church asked only the question: What is right? But when in the 4th century persecution of the church ended and when Christianity later became politically legitimized as the official state religion in most of Europe, and few believed that the end of the world was just around the corner, the church had to ask the other question: What is good? This created a series of questions: What are the consequences of *not* going to war in certain circumstances? How does one protect the innocent from oppression and injustice? In what way is the Christian responsible for the larger welfare of society? Pacifism was no longer an easy or obvious answer.

The result was the development of the doctrine of "just war," which has for centuries formed the mainstream of Christian tradition and influenced international law theory. The criteria used to judge whether or not a given armed conflict is "just" are usually divided into two parts: the *jus ad bellum* principles regarding the moral justification for resorting to war; and the *jus in bello* principles regarding morally permissible conduct in fighting a war. The following are recognized "just war" principles. (The first five are *jus ad bellum* and the remaining two *jus in bello* principles.)

1. War must be declared by legitimate authority.
2. There must be a justifiable cause.
3. War must be entered into with the right intention (i.e., a morally justifiable end).
4. War must be a last resort.
5. There must be a reasonable hope of success.
6. Armed force must be used with discrimination, especially between directly and intentionally attacking combatants or military objectives (permissible), and directly and intentionally attacking non-combatants or non-military targets (impermissible).
7. The amount of armed force used must be proportionate to the end sought (i.e., the value of the objective sought must outweigh the harm done in seeking it).

Traditionally, a carefully prescribed set of limits and conditions was theoretically considered before armed force was thought morally justified. Self-defense was generally considered a legitimate reason for using force, although even in this case a close relationship between the amount of force used and the end sought was believed essential. These "just war" criteria are often misunderstood. They do not seek to legitimize the use of armed force. Their purpose, rather, is to avoid war except as a last resort, and then to limit the use of armed force even in pursuit of justifiable purposes.

This traditional moral doctrine on warfare, part of early Christian thought, is applicable but inadequate for the nuclear age. The moral and ethical implications of nuclear weapons carry a profoundly different challenge. Nuclear weapons have broken the bounds of classical strategic and political thought, and by their inherent destructiveness they present an unacceptable risk that any nuclear war would be a war without limits. They render meaningless traditional standards of discrimination; they destroy the proportionality between means and ends that was traditionally appealed to in ethical arguments. Paul Ramsey, for example, stands almost alone among ethicists in arguing that measures of discrimination, proportionality, and intention can be preserved in the use of nuclear weapons by choosing targets prudently and aiming carefully.[2] Such arguments seem like ethical gymnastics to us. We have difficulty visualizing how nuclear exchanges can produce limited damage when major population centers lie near military targets and when the command and control of such exchanges is itself likely to be destroyed.

We are particularly disturbed by the argument that counterforce targeting is "more moral" than targeting cities. This argument states that although collateral damage may be very great, it is morally excusable because it is unintended. We reject this argument. If one knows that terrible and long-lasting destruction will occur unavoidably, and accepts that, then "unintendedness" has no meaning.

The committee believes that the right of self-defense — and that extends to national defense — is recognized in Christian theology and tradition. We understand the perspective of Christian pacifism, and accept it as a personal option for those who for reasons of individual conscience embrace and exercise it. And we acknowledge that the pacifist tradition still provides a challenge to the church when it reminds us that the ethics of a just war are themselves rooted in the conviction that warfare is sinful and morally unacceptable. We believe, however, that a distinction must be drawn between pacifism as a personal

<hr />

[2] See Paul Ramsey, *The Just War: Force and Political Responsibility*, New York: Scribner, 1968.

option, and pacifism as public policy. The majority of the committee do not support the latter.

We also recognize as legitimate the perspective of non-violent resistance, and accept it as a personal option and as a possible collective approach to conflict resolution. Indeed, the committee believes that it is a course of conduct that needs to be thought about more fully. We are honestly troubled, however, by the claim that non-violent resistance can be effective in settling conflicts between nations. Most of us have difficulty seeing how it meets the responsibility to protect the innocent from oppression's spread, or to prevent suffering, although we understand it as a valid means of resisting internal oppression and injustice. Non-violent resistance was indeed successfully used as a means to achieve human and civil rights in the United States during the 1960's.

Nuclear Weapons, Deterrence and Morality

As detailed in the previous chapters, the committee does not believe that any limits can or would be set on the conduct of nuclear war, nor do we see any strategy for the use of such weapons on a limited basis, no matter what the technological improvements. Weapons from our strategic arsenals used against city targets (or military targets near cities) would violate the criterion of discrimination; and large numbers of strategic weapons used against military targets would cause vast collateral damage and violate the rules of proportionality. As mentioned, even tactical weapons used on European soil would cause disproportionate damage around densely populated areas and would carry a risk of triggering larger responses leading to widespread destruction. The use of nuclear force, therefore, would in our view end up creating devastation disproportionate to the political end for which it was initiated.

This theoretical consideration leads to a more practical and immediate dilemma. If peace is maintained through the fear of the use of nuclear weapons, will not a moral condemnation of such use undermine the deterrent consequences of nuclear stalemate? If their use is condemned, should we not also condemn the threat to use them? And if so, does this weaken deterrence, whose consequences have been good? Can one rationally say, "possession yes; use, no?" These questions fall right in the middle of the moral tension between what is right and what is good.

We asked ourselves, first, whether deterrence ceases to exist if one possesses nuclear weapons but decides, for whatever reasons, to foreswear their use. Some experts argue that it does. Deterrence is not inherent in the weapons, they maintain, but in the combination of possession and the willingness to use them. Thus, when the will is removed, deterrence is vitiated. We do not agree with that. In considerable measure, deterrence is indeed inherent in the nature of the weapons. Their very existence gives both sides pause because they simply do not know if the weapons will be used, nor what would happen if they are used. It is this uncertainty about what would happen in an actual confrontation, rather than the certainty as to intention, that creates deterrence. The committee found, therefore, considerable validity in the concept of "existential deterrence," a phrase first used by McGeorge Bundy:

> The terrible and unavoidable uncertainties in any recourse to nuclear war create what could be called 'existential' deterrence, where the function of the adjective is to distinguish this phenomenon from anything based on strategic theories or declared policies or even international commitments. As long as each side has large numbers of thermonuclear weapons that *could* be used against the opponent, even after the strongest possible preemptive attack, existential deterrence is strong and it rests on uncertainty about what could happen. . . . Now that both strategic arsenals are redundantly destructive and amply survivable, we can say with still more confidence that existential deterrence is strong and that its strength is essentially independent of most changes in deployment.[3]

[3] Quoted in "The Bishops and the Bomb," *New York Review of Books*, June 16, 1983, p. 4.

In our view, therefore, deterrence results primarily from the *existence* of nuclear weapons, not on elaborate plans for their use. The notion that if deterrence fails nuclear weapons can be used to fight and outlast the enemy is a delusion. The accompanying premise that the best deterrent is a nuclear war-fighting capability is equally a delusion, and is unacceptable to us. The more ambitious the nuclear war-fighting strategy, the greater the illusion that control can be maintained. Deterrence, in our view, is a simple concept that says nuclear weapons exist but they must not be used because once used they run the risk of destroying both sides. Deterrence paradoxically depends on a threat that must never be carried out. A clear distinction can be made between deterrence and use, and deterrence does not depend on an explicitly defined threat of use.

How does one view, ethically and morally, the possession of weapons with the implicit threat and uncertainty that they may be used if a nation is attacked? The committee's deliberations on this point went something like this: We accept the intrinsic moral wrongness of using nuclear weapons. We are, however, not persuaded that it is in the same sense absolutely wrong to hold them for the purpose of deterring the Soviet Union. We realize that there are serious moral ambiguities in this position.

The committee accepts the act of possession simply because the need to prevent nuclear war forces us to do so. For some it is a lesser evil; for others a moral responsibility in a broken world; for still others an interim necessity on a course toward the abolition of nuclear weapons; and for all the recognition that there are no sinless policies in a sinful world. Even if there is only a probable chance that nuclear war will be prevented the deterrent effect of holding weapons in the present nuclear stalemate, then that aim would seem to have an overriding claim on a responsible government, notwithstanding its inevitable moral cost. To refuse on moral grounds to adopt a position that prevents nuclear war seems to us to be a precarious moral position.

From this base, the committee considered questions that the Christian might raise. Is the use of nuclear weapons to be condemned without qualification? Is there no circumstance and no condition under which any use, however limited, would be morally justified? Would one ever "push the button"? And for what? More specifically, would the use of nuclear weapons be justified to preserve American freedoms?

None of the members of the committee could imagine any circumstances in which deliberately initiating the use of nuclear weapons could be morally justified. We hold this view, after the most careful deliberation, because we do not believe that the use of nuclear weapons could terminate a conventional conflict with a comparably armed adversary, and because we believe that it would be extraordinarily difficult to stop a nuclear war once it has started.

Should the United States then publicly rule out the first use of nuclear weapons ahead of time? The committee divided on this question. Some believed that the United States should take the moral high ground, and proclaim publicly that the U.S. will not use nuclear weapons. They also felt that any such declaration would not weaken deterrence, since uncertainty would continue to restrain use, and since the Soviets would probably no more believe this declaration than we believe their no-first-use pledge. Other members of the committee opposed any public no-first-use declaration, feeling that it is important to maximize uncertainty. They also felt that such a declaration would disturb our alliance relationships. Over the past four decades, the United States has stressed, and our allies have accepted, the concept of first use of nuclear weapons to protect their security. Any change in this policy — even if it would be desirable — should be made only after careful deliberation and preparation with our allies.

What about second use of nuclear weapons in response to another nation's initial use? The committee again divided. Some members of the committee felt that they could not imagine every theoretically possible contingency or condition, and therefore could not disavow every conceivable use. They could not, in other words, exclude the possibility that some narrow use — for example, to terminate hostilities — might prevent a greater evil. Others on the committee simply felt that the use of nuclear weapons was intrinsically wrong, and that one had to say "no" at some point.

What we face is a tragic moral dilemma in which no resolution is possible that does not contain risk or moral cost. No option exists that we can espouse with an easy conscience. Some would threaten to use nuclear weapons, and make the sole criterion for their policy whether that would make nuclear war less likely. We do not believe that this can be the sole criterion. One needs to strike a balance between the deterrent aim of policy and the "moral cost" of relying on the nuclear threat. We need to combine moral sensitivity with prudential judgment. The two cannot be separated. Indeed, public debate creates the danger of polarized views, and as one philosopher/ theologian wrote: "[morally] sensitive people may be led to think they need not be responsible, and, worse still, that responsible people may feel they need not be [morally] sensitive."[4]

The committee concludes that it is morally acceptable to possess nuclear weapons for the purpose of deterrence, understanding the implicit and uncertain dangers that they may be used. We take this view because we see no other acceptable way to reduce the likelihood of nuclear war at this time. We are bound by the logic of mutual vulnerability, and we cannot escape it or survive by acting as if it did not exist or by destroying its axioms.

To argue that deterrence is acceptable is not to argue that it is desirable, or that it must be permanent. It is all that we can do now, in the face of an objective condition we cannot unilaterally change. No system or situation is satisfactory, however, which cannot survive a failure of machine or human intelligence. To argue, as balance-of-power proponents sometimes do, that we must balance power and competitiveness

[4] Basil Mitchell, "The Church and the Bomb," in David Martin and Peter Mullen, eds., *Unholy Warfare: The Church and the and Bomb,* Oxford: Basil Blackwell Publishers, 1984.

precariously forever, is to let the present condition become steadily more dangerous. The trend toward nuclear war-fighting capabilities and strategic defenses that have a distinctly offensive character bodes ill over the long term. The current condition must evolve into something more sturdy and safe. The task before us, both morally and prudentially, is to move carefully away from dependence on nuclear deterrence, while recognizing its current necessity.

This brings us to the matter of "controlling vision." As we have said, the Gospel compels us to admit that with nuclear weapons we are talking about something essentially wrong. The committee feels a deep unease over humanity's coexistence with these weapons. Our controlling vision — expressing scripture, tradition, and reason — requires us to move from a greater to lesser reliance on these weapons, to the reduction and management of the tensions between the superpowers, and to better political relationships in the world.

We understand that we are speaking here of a long time period. But decisions made today will be different if the controlling vision is to move away from reliance on nuclear weapons rather than a vision of anticipation and preparation for nuclear war. What is important at this point is not a precise long-range blueprint, but the intention and the direction in which we are moving, and in which we wish to move. What is also important is the determination to move in that right and moral direction.

Neither practitioners of *real politik* nor moral perfectionists will be satisfied with the considerations we have laid out here. The practitioners will argue that international politics are amoral, that the search for power always takes precedence over the search for reason and good will, and that trying to express or observe values only impedes the necessary self-interest of nations. The perfectionists may fault us for failing to repudiate nuclear weapons out of hand. We understand their outrage, but the urge to repudiate the weapons simply to have clean hands gave way, in our view, to the need to grasp the current issues and sort them out. Morally and prudentially, our need was to derive politically feasible alternatives, not merely damn the current situation and walk away.

Loving One's Enemies

Most of the public debate about nuclear weapons, whether in ethical, political, or military terms, reflects essentially a fear about survival. Self-preservation and survival are legitimate concerns, of course. But in the nuclear age, survival and self-preservation are intimately linked to a question that stems from the very roots of Christian morality: How ought we, as followers of Christ, to love our enemies?

One cannot deny that the teachings and life of Jesus as portrayed in Scripture place loving one's enemies as a fundamental concern. Reconciliation is a central issue and obligation for Christians. As one theologian has written, the nature of our love for enemies "may be the litmus test for assessing our Christian authenticity."[5] The logic of Christian reconciliation is that each human being is the object of God's love. Our "enemy" is also the brother or sister for whom Christ died. We are undoubtedly someone's enemy. In the phrasing of David Duke, who strongly influenced our thinking on this issue, enemies lose their enemy status in light of the cross. All of us stand around that cross, and all of us have in some way contributed to that crucifixion. As Dietrich Bonhoeffer wrote:

> In the face of the cross the disciples realized that they too were His enemies, and that He had overcome them by His love. It is this that opens the disciple's eyes and enables him to see his enemy as a brother.[6]

Christ's call for us to love our enemies, moreover, involves no promise that loving enemies will change them. Bonhoeffer again illuminates this:

> Jesus does not promise that when we bless our enemies and do good to them they will not despitefully use and persecute us.... By our enemies Jesus means

[5] David N. Duke, "Christians, Enemies and Nuclear Weapons," *The Christian Century*, November 2, 1983, pp. 986-989.
[6] Dietrich Bonhoeffer, *The Cost of Discipleship*, New York: Macmillan, 1959, pp. 166-167.

those who are quite intractable and utterly unrespon-
sive to our love, who forgive us nothing when we forgive them all, who requite love with hatred and our
service with derision.[7]

This drives home the Christian's dilemma. How can one restrain evil, preserve good, or defend the innocent with a
method that may not "work?" Is Christ's injunction qualified
in any way by its practical efficacy in specific circumstances?

The nub of the problem, of course, is that this is an extremely
difficult, demanding — some would say "unnatural"— injunction. Human nature, after all, is deeply self-oriented and at best
"tribal" oriented. Selfishness, self-love, and vindictiveness are
the traits of our fallen nature. The visceral reflex of most people is to "crush" enemies, not accept them; to pursue security
by seeking to dominate others. Here it is useful to reflect on
the evolving tradition of the Judeo-Christian heritage regarding enemies and how to respond to them. The Old Testament
clearly shows a growing recognition by the Hebrew prophets
and historians that an enemy is also God's creature. In the older
records of Hebrew experience, God is the one who rescues the
chosen people by frustrating or destroying their enemies (Exo-
dus 15:6; Numbers 10:9). If the faithful are oppressed, they call
on God to rescue them (Psalm 7:6). But there is also an understanding that if the Hebrews do not live up to their covenant
with God, they will be punished for their wrongdoing (I Kings
8:33 Lamentations 1:8,9), and that God will even choose an enemy to be the instrument or rod of God's purposes. Finally, there
comes a slow and reluctant recognition that the enemy has
some basic values and rights in God's eyes. Solomon is com-
mended for not asking God to destroy God's enemies (I Kings
3:11), and a Hebrew proverb advises the faithful not to relish
their enemies' misfortunes (Proverbs 24:17) because God may
change and come to their rescue. The Book of Jonah also illus-
trates this point very compellingly. In Proverbs the author argues that hungry and thirsty enemies should be fed, if only

[7] *Ibid.*, pp. 166-167.

to induce them to reform their ways (Proverbs 25:21). In the New Testament, the universal nature of Christ's teaching and salvation reflects the earlier doctrine of creation, wherein all of humanity is recognized as being made in the image of God. No one is truly faithful to the Hebrew covenants in Christ's eyes, and all fall short of God's expectations. Hence, reconciliation with, rather than destruction of, one's adversary is taught, and wherever possible we are to agree with our adversary quickly (Matthew 5:25). Christ's command to "love your enemy" (Matthew 5:44), which in its context probably referred to interpersonal relations, also reveals a general attitude and spirit. Finally, on the cross Christ asked for God to forgive those who killed Him (Luke 23:34). Hence His followers were to be concerned for the spiritual and material welfare of all, friends and enemies alike. Such a concern could still lead both individuals and nations to self-defense — a truth that the Church recognized when its members began in the 4th century to assume responsibility for government. The primary goal, however, was to be at peace with one's adversaries and to seek reconciliation with them rather than their destruction.

It seemed to the committee, as we struggled with these concepts and ideas, that Christ's redemptive ministry compels us to accept reconciliation as an essential element of our "controlling vision" in public policy, despite our imperfect and inefficient efforts, and however antagonistic and intractable our adversaries may be. We concur with the report of the National Joint Commission on Peace of the Episcopal Church, which addressed the issue:

> To love our nation's enemies is today as difficult as it is urgent. Nevertheless, to avoid dehumanizing stereotypes, to see to it that what peacetime good we do is done impartially, to champion justice self-critically on our side of any growing hostilities, and even in hostilities to continue doing good to those who may hate us, these are specific and concrete actions, clearly expected of us according to scripture... They describe an attitude, a perspective, an intentionality which

should inform our actions toward enemies, even in the midst of conflict when the possibilities for peace and reconciliation seem most remote.[8]

To love our enemies in the nuclear era, therefore, will mean certain things to the Christian. Understanding is one form of love: the understanding of our enemies' history, culture, needs, prejudices, geographical constrictions, profound beliefs. Love also implies familiarity, personal encounters with those who hold such "enemy" beliefs. Love may not directly transform institutional hostilities into amicable relations, but love can and traditionally has informed and enriched human interactions from which institutional behavior derives. To that end, therefore, in both personal and public life, the Christian urgently but patiently must be an "ambassador for Christ," a bearer of reconciling love in the world, daring to be at peace with others as God in Christ has made a full and reconciling peace with us.

[8] Report of the Joint Commission on Peace, *op. cit.*, pp 9-10.

Epilogue: A Policy Ethic

To study one subject intensively over an extended period of time with the same group of colleagues, as we have done, is bound to be a moving and personally significant experience. Only a few of us began this endeavor with any particular knowledge or background in nuclear issues. Most of us were unfamiliar with the basics, and not a little apprehensive at the formidable nature of the subject. While none of us now pretends to "expert level" technical or strategic knowledge, all of us have been able, through this process of study and discussion, to grasp the fundamentals, deal with the arguments, and understand the current public dialogue. We are not now so easily intimidated by technical jargon and selective reasoning. The process of rubbing minds together, like shining a flashlight into dark corners, has illuminated what had earlier seemed forbidding.

We have come to realize that quite practical issues of politics and power lie underneath all of the technical esoterica. We were impressed with how closely these specialized questions of technology, military strategy and geopolitics are connected to the fundamental stuff of human nature—power, fear and egoism. How true is the old adage that "everything is part of everything else."

We were struck as well by a persistent background factor which seems to us sufficiently disturbing to warrant special note here: namely, the degree of self-delusion and "game playing" into which participants in these matters are tempted. Since Hiroshima and Nagasaki, the world has no real experience with nuclear warfare, so we lack empirical evidence regarding a whole range of vital questions. As a consequence, theories, assumptions and beliefs tend to create the "reality" framework in which this subject is discussed. In such circumstances, biases and self-interest often drive reasoning.

This raises the clear danger that strategic theories may be built on illusion or misperception, as we noted in the comments on "superiority" in chapter III. Even when analysts understand this, however, they find it terribly hard to declare that the Emperor has no clothes.

More insidious is what George Orwell called "political language" — the deliberate misuse or misrepresentation of facts and arguments. "Political language," Orwell wrote, "is designed to make lies sound truthful and murder respectable, and to give an appearance of solidity to pure wind."[1] We were deeply disturbed by the numerous assertions of a reality for which no solid basis exists, but which have become conventional wisdom by endless repetition. All of the "gaps," from the bomber gap of the 1950's to the "window of vulnerability" of the 1980's, are of this genre, as is the flat assertion that the United States is strategically inferior to the Soviet Union.

We were also startled to realize how easily people professionally involved in the nuclear problem can insulate themselves from the flesh and blood meaning and consequences of their own actions and recommendations through the use of euphemistic language. How easily, for example, defense analysts write "scenarios," setting forth actions of great or dire consequences, as if they were writing a fictional movie script. Pain and difficulty are avoided by analogy and euphemism. As Orwell noted, "If thought can corrupt language, language can also corrupt thought."[2]

These points are not frivolous. We make them to underscore a major proposition: Careful and continuous public scrutiny of experts and expertise is an absolute necessity in the area of nuclear weapons and strategy. Proposals for new policies and weapons systems must not be accepted uncritically. The reasoning put forth must be examined rigorously and skeptically.[3]

We came to the end of our inquiry, then, fully convinced of the validity of the assumption with which we began: That

[1] George Orwell, "Politics and the English Language," in *The Orwell Reader*, Richard H. Rovere, ed., New York: Harcourt, Brace, Jovanovich, Inc., 1956, p. 364.

[2] Orwell, *op.cit.*, p 361.

[3] *Voter Options on Nuclear Arms Policy*, Public Agenda Foundation, *op.cit.*, documents differences between what it calls the public's "common sense" and the professionals' expert opiniion, pp. 8—9.

the average person can understand and reach sound conclusions on nuclear policy questions — and has a civic obligation to do so.

A Policy Ethic.

In confronting the world, Christians face their own particular dilemma. On the one hand, New Testament scripture calls for love of God and love of neighbor. As members in the Body of Christ, we are called to be ministers of reconciliation and service. On the other hand, we live in a world driven by the considerations of self-preservation, self-interest, power, prejudice, even hate. International politics and the "game of states" — their quest for power, their search for unilateral advantage, their rivalry, their insecurity — are realities which will not go away.

To argue that moral behavior in international affairs is impossible or to grant states a selective morality profoundly different from traditional norms of ethical behavior does not resolve the dilemma. From a prudential standpoint alone, the claims of ordinary morality, the clamor for state conduct that is not predominantly characterized by violence and deceit, are irrepressible. States, after all, are led by human beings. Their actions affect human beings within and outside their nations, and often in life and death ways. Considerations of good and evil, right and wrong, are both legitimate and unavoidable. Christians can certainly not avoid such matters. The stern, even revolutionary demands of the Gospel, and the imperatives of their faith, provide them with a mandate to regard their discipleship as relevant to their role as political beings.

All of this is rendered crucial by the nuclear dilemma. There is simply no precedent for the challenge that nuclear weapons presents to our physical and moral lives. Each of us is inescapably involved in the nuclear dilemma. We are targets or victims. In a democracy, we are also taxpayers and voters and thus participants in policymaking. How do we — as citizens in a democracy — carry on moral discourse and carry out Christian witness with regard to a subject that seems so intractable a challenge?

However, we have found that the application of moral thought to human behavior has to be considered in terms of different domains and contexts. In terms of moral and ethical obligations and opportunities, there is a difference between an individual and a corporate entity, such as a government. Individual moral maxims cannot be directly transposed to a corporate level, as we noted in the preceding chapter. A political leader or statesman has a responsibility for the welfare of others, and must act for the collective good. He is not morally entitled to sacrifice their interests. As a leader he is not free to act in the way he might as an individual. There is also a marked difference between domestic and international politics. An identifiable sense of community exists at the national level which permits the formal definition of rights and obligations. A national government provides a framework of social order within the social order. Institutions exist able to legislate, adjudicate and manage competing claims.

At the international level, such legal, social and institutional framework as exists is still rudimentary. There is only a limited consensus among the sovereign states, such as in the United Nations system, and there is no common sovereign above them. There are competing philosophies and clashing cultural traditions.

The absence of moral standards in relations among states, however, does not relieve statesmen of the obligation of moral choice. It only makes their task more complicated. The Hobbesian view of international politics as a natural state of constant warring is not a completely accurate picture. States are not always competing against each other all the time everywhere, nor does the competition always and everywhere involve the issue of national survival. The Machiavellian concept that any act in the national interest is by definition moral and acceptable is both inaccurate and inadequate. The need of states to survive and to defend their interests does not mean that only selfish acts are possible.

In our view, not only do such "realist" concepts fail to define the realities; they also do not provide wise policy for our time. They are not compatible with our survival. Moral choice in foreign policy is a practical requirement for survival in the nuclear age.

How do we define moral choice in foreign policy? What kind of ethic must statecraft follow? Here we refer back to the four ethical tests of ends, means, motives and consequences, described in chapter VI. The assessment of facts, the weighing of uncertainties and the determination of options must be measured against all four dimensions. Adequate policy in our time must also be guided by the imperative to move international relations away from the characteristics of the jungle toward a more just world. What might this mean in practical terms? We found no more trenchant formulation than Stanley Hoffman's prescription:

> We need a statecraft that stresses long-term collective gains rather than short or long-term national advantages; that accepts the need for a large measure of institutionalization in international affairs, and for important commitments of resources to common enterprises; that shows great restraint in its use of means; and that goes, in its choice of ends, far beyond the realm of interstate relations.[4]

This controlling vision contrasts starkly with the relatively weak international institutions at present. Still there exists a fairly wide "sense of humanity," that we can build upon. What is now required, in our view, is the progressive development of an overarching moral ethic that transcends particular value systems associated with particular groups and states. *That* is what the insights of religion and theology provide. To Christians, it is the transcendence of God; the fact that humans are the clearest reflection of God's presence in the world; the biblical proclamation that in Christ we are neither Jew nor Greek, but all one in Him — it is these things that provide the foundation and the possibility for constructing the sense of universal

---

[4] Stanley Hoffman, *Duties Beyond Borders*, Syracuse, N.Y.: Syracuse University Press, 1981, p. 205.

community that can underpin the policy ethic and statecraft required for survival in the nuclear era. Hope is born of faith in God and the knowledge that Christ is the Lord of History. In this hope and faith, people facing their political responsibilities may discover new courage to refrain from futile trust in violence to maintain or extend the national or universal interest, and from self-regard, prejudice and hate. Christians in our day place too low an estimate on the power which reconciliation could have if practiced by nations. And they do so because they have been saturated with political and military doctrines and conventional wisdom that engender cynicism and rob them of the courage to invoke these deeper truths of redemptive love.

We have prepared and distributed this report on the nuclear dilemma with a deep sense of our own unworthiness, our little faith, our halting obedience, but also with an abiding belief that in response to faith, God will now, as in other times of human sinning and despair, impart new light and ower to His church and His people. If we were truly to believe what we say and sing each Sunday; if we were as a consequence truly to become the agents of God's purpose in the world; if we were able thereby to infuse political decision making with the kind of statecraft referred to and the kind of compassion and redemptive love we are called upon to display — if all this were possible — then Christian citizenship would indeed acquire a new meaning and become a channel of grace and renewal for the world.

Acknowledgments

No enterprise of this sort can succeed without the assistance and cooperation of a large number of people. We wish to express our appreciation to all of those throughout the Diocese of Washington and beyond who have helped us and encouraged us. They are so numerous we could not, practically, list each by name. We do feel compelled, however, to single out a few.

Viron P. Vaky, Chairman

The Rt. Rev. John T. Walker, Bishop of Washington, for giving us the opportunity to carry out this study. He encouraged us, urged us to let our consciences take us where they would, and permitted us to carry out our work without preconditions, constraints, or limitations of any kind. We hope the results have justified his trust.

The Rev. Canon Charles Martin, Chairman of the Commission on Peace, who, as *ex officio* member of the Committee of Inquiry, participated faithfully and actively in our deliberations and contributed substantively to them. His wisdom, faith, and dedication spurred us on and encouraged us along the way.

Mary Ellen Holbrook, of the staff of the Washington Cathedral, whom we shamelessley appropriated as our *de facto* secretary. Without her energy, efficiency and dedication in taking care of our mailings, document reproductions, administrative arrangements, and her general back-up support, we could never have finished our task. The grace with which she accomodated our impositions on her time and regular work was surely above and beyond the call of duty.

Michael Krepon, Senior Associate of the Carnegie Endowment for International Peace, who served as the committee's staff consultant. His expertise and patience were indispensable in guiding us through the intricacies of the nuclear issue, and in providing us with a realistic understanding of the history and nature of the various questions one must face. The committee's conclusions and opinions, however, are our own; they do not necessarily reflect his.

Stephen Wrage, Visiting Professor, U.S. Naval Academy, who served as our Rapporteur. His meticulous and thorough reports provided us with a permanent record which we could review and refer to in the course of our deliberations. His work also enabled those of us who could not attend every meeting to keep fully up to date with the pace of our inquiry, and his assistance in other aspects of our writing and editing was a major contribution to the completion of our work.

Robert L. McCan, Associate Director, Institute for Space and Security Studies; former associate for research and development, Center for Theology and Public Policy, who — with Dr. Alan Geyer — prepared special material for our study on the ethical/theological setting. A faithful and active member of the Committee of Inquiry itself, his "extra" work in providing us with background and analytical material and in guiding us in this area was an essential contribution to our endeavor.

Anne Shirk, Staff Associate, Commission on Peace. Hardworking and dedicated, she spent many long, patient hours with the committee helping us organize our thoughts and preparing and revising the many texts that issued from our deliberations. She also acted as liaison between the Committee of Inquiry and the Diocesan Commission on Peace.

Committee of Inquiry

Viron P. Vaky, Chairman Senior Associate, Carnegie Endowment for International Peace. Former Assistant Secretary of State for Inter-American Affairs, and Ambassador to Colombia, Venezuela, and Costa Rica. Member, St. Luke's Church, Bethesda, MD.

H. Albion Ferrell Clergy Assistant, Retired, St. Luke's Church, Washington, DC.

Charles W. Gilchrist Postulant for Holy Orders; Former Executive of Montgomery County, Maryland. Member, St. Luke's Church, Bethesda, MD.

Michael P. Hamilton Canon, The Washington Cathedral.

Townsend Hoopes Director, American Committee on U.S.-Soviet Relations. Former Undersecretary of the Air Force. Author, *The Limits of Intervention* (Vietnam) and *The Devil and John Foster Dulles*.

Fisher Howe Management consultant; Retired Foreign Service Officer. Member, St. John's Church, Lafayette Square, Washington, DC.

Nancy Ignatius President, National Cathedral Association. Member, Cathedral Chapter.

John Karefa-Smart, M.D. Consultant, primary health care and international health program; member, International Physicians for the Prevention of Nuclear War. Former Assistant Director General, World Health Organization. Member, St. Augustine's Church, Washington, DC.

Carol Laise Former Director General of the Foreign Service, and Ambassador to Nepal. Member, St. John's Church, Georgetown Parish, Washington, DC.

Edward L. Lee, Jr. Rector, St. John's Church, Georgetown Parish, Washington, DC.

John D. LeRoy, Jr. Standing Committee, Diocese of Washington. Senior Warden Emeritus, Trinity Church, St. Mary's City, MD.

Robert Gerald Livingston Director, American Institute for Contemporary German Studies, The Johns Hopkins University. Former member, the National Security Council staff, and the U.S. Foreign Service. Member, St. Paul's Church, Rock Creek Parish, Washington, DC.

Robert L. McCan Associate Director, Institute for Space and Security Studies. Member, St. Augustine's Church, Washington, DC.

Hope Moore Former Commissioner of Parks, Libraries, Cultural and International Affairs, Atlanta. Former Associate Director of Cultural Programs, Carter Administration.

Lorin R. Stieff Former member, Arms Control and Disarmament Agency. Member, All Saints' Church, Chevy Chase, MD.

John G. Womack Assistant Chief Counsel, National Highway Traffic Safety Administration. Former member, Standing Committee, Diocese of Washington. Member, St. Columba's Church, Washington, DC.

Ex Officio

The Rt. Rev. John T. Walker Bishop of Washington

The Rev. Canon Charles Martin Chairman, Commission on Peace, Episcopal Diocese of Washington

Adjunct Staff

Mary Ellen Holbrook Washington Cathedral Staff

Michael Krepon Senior Associate, Carnegie Endowment for International Peace

Anne Shirk Staff Associate, Commission on Peace

Stephen Wrage Visiting Professor, U.S. Naval Academy

Witnesses

Kenneth Adelman Director, the U.S. Arms Control and Disarmament Agency.

Barry Blechman President, Defense Forecasts, Inc. Formerly Assistant Director of the Arms Control and Disarmament Agency and Director of Defense studies at the Brookings Institution.

Colin Burch Colonel, U.S. Air Force (Ret.); Member, All Saints' Church.

Richard Burt U.S. Ambassador to West Germany. Former Assistant Secretary of State for European Affairs; former defense correspondent for *The New York Times.*

Barry Carter Vice President of the Arms Control Association; former NSC staff member under President Nixon with responsibility for SALT, NATO and U.S. Soviet issues.

Lillian Daniels Member, Church of the Redeemer, Bethesda, MD.

Robert Dean Deputy Assistant Director, Bureau of Politico- Military Affairs, U.S. Department of State.

Norman Dicks Member, House of Representatives (D-Washington) serving on the Defense Appropriations Subcommittee.

Alton Frye Washington Director of the Council on Foreign Relations.

Richard Garwin IBM Fellow, Thomas J. Watson Research Center; Professor of Physics at Cornell and Columbia; former member of the President's Science Advisory Commission.

Noel Gayler Admiral, U.S. Navy (Ret.); Former Commander-in- Chief, Pacific, Deputy Director of the Joint Strategic Targeting Planning Staff, and Director of the National Security Agency.

Leslie Gelb Defense correspondent for *The New York Times*; Former Director of the Bureau of Politico- Military Affairs, U.S. Department of State.

John M. Gessell Professor Emeritus of Christian Ethics, The School of Theology of The University of the South, Sewanee, Tennessee.

Robert Gessert Program director with the Logistics Management Institute.

Alan Geyer Executive Director, the Center for Theology and Public Policy and author of *The Idea of Disarmament*.

Dana Grubb Charter member of the Washington Chapter of the Episcopal Peace Fellowship; member, St. Anne's Church, Damascus, MD.

Morton Halperin Director of the Center for National Security Studies; Director, Legislative Office, American Civil Liberties Union; former Deputy Assistant Secretary of Defense (1966-1969) and Senior staff member of the NSC (1969); and author of *Limited War in the Nuclear Age*.

Bryan Hehir, S.J. Secretary of the Department of Social Development and World Peace, U.S. Catholic Conference; Senior Research Scholar, Kennedy Institute of Ethics; Research Professor of Ethics and International Politics of the Foreign Service, Georgetown University; principal drafter of "A Pastoral Letter on War and Peace."

Elizabeth Holmes-Vilar Former Director of the Episcopal Peace Fellowship.

William Hyland Editor, *Foreign Affairs*; former Deputy Director of the National Security Council staff, 1975-1977.

John A. Jamieson Former Assistant Director of the Ballistic Missile Defense Agency; Member, Church of the Redeemer, Bethesda, MD.

David Jones General, U.S. Air Force (ret.); Chairman of the Joint Chiefs of Staff under Presidents Carter and Reagan.

John Karefa-Smart, M.D. Member of the Committee of Inquiry and International Physicians for the Prevention of Nuclear War. Former Assistant Director of the World Health Organization.

Michael Krepon Staff Consultant to the Committee of Inquiry and Senior Associate at the Carnegie Endowment for International Peace, formerly Director of Defense Program and Policy Reviews, U.S. Arms Control and Disarmament Agency.

Jack Matlock U.S. Ambassador to the Soviet Union; former Senior Specialist in Soviet and East European Affairs at the National Security Council, formerly Deputy Chief of Mission and Charge d'Affaires in Moscow and Ambassador to Czechoslovakia.

Tillie Muller Member, Church of the Redeemer, Bethesda, MD.

Paul Nitze Special Representative for Arms Control and Disarmament Negotiations; former Secretary of the Navy, Deputy Secretary of Defense; Chief of the U.S. Delegations to the Intermediate Range Nuclear Forces Negotiations.

Joseph Nye Professor, Kennedy School of Government, Harvard University; former Deputy Undersecretary of State for Security Assistance in the Carter Administration.

Allen Parrent Professor of Theology and Ethics at Virginia Theological Seminary.

Charles Perry Provost, The Washington Cathedral.

Robert Pirie Assistant Secretary of Defense for Manpower, the Carter Administration. Member, St.John's Church, Lafayette Square, Washington, DC.

Frederick Ruth Ambassador of the Federal Republic of Germany to Italy; former Commissioner of Germany for Arms Control and Disarmament.

David Scott Professor of Theology and Ethics at Virginia Theological Seminary.

Roger Shinn Reinhold Niebuhr Professor of Social Ethics at Union Theological Seminary, New York.

Dimitri Simes Senior Associate at the Carnegie Endowment for International Peace; Consultant to the Arms Control and Disarmament Agency.

Walter Slocombe Former chairman of the Department of Defense SALT Task Force and Deputy Undersecretary of Defense for Policy Planning in the Carter administration.

Gerard Smith Chief of U.S. negotiating team at SALT (1969-1972) and Ambassador-at-Large and Special Presidential Representative for Nonproliferation Matters (1977-1980); author of *Double-talk: the Story of SALT I.*

John Walker Bishop of the Episcopal Diocese of Washington.

Jim Wallis Founder and head of "Sojourners," a prophetic community dedicated to worship and witness on public policy issues including the arms race.

Catharine Ward Founder of the Virginia Chapter of the Episcopal Peace Fellowship and member at St. Augustine's Church, Washington, DC.

Paul Warnke Former Director, Arms Control and Disarmament Agency (1977-1978) and chief of the U.S. negotiating team at SALT II.

Caspar Weinberger U.S. Secretary of Defense.

John Wheeler President, The Project on the Vietnam Generation; chaired Vietnam Veterans' Memorial Fund.

Jack Woodard Rector, Meade Memorial Episcopal Church, Alexandria, VA.

Glossary
of Technical Terms

air-launched missile—See cruise missile.

anti-ballistic missile (ABM) system—A system of missiles and radars capable of defending against a ballistic-missile attack by destroying incoming offensive missiles. The defensive missiles may be armed with either nuclear or non-nuclear warheads.

anti-satellite (ASAT)—An abbreviation for an anti-satellite weapon.

arms control—Any unilateral action or multilateral plan, arrangement, or process, resting upon explicit or implicit international agreement, which limits or regulates any aspect of the following: the production, numbers, type configuration, and performance characteristics of weapon systems (including related command and control, logistics support, and intelligence arrangements or mechanisms); and the numerical strength, organization, equipment, deployment or employment of the armed forces retained by the parties.

ballistic missile—A missile, classified by range, that moves on a free-falling trajectory under the influence of gravity.

ballistic missile defense (BMD)—See ABM system.

bomber—An aircraft, usually classified by range, capable of delivering nuclear and non-nuclear ordnance. Long-range bombers are those capable of traveling 6000 or more miles on one load of fuel; medium-range bombers can travel between 3500 and 6000 miles without refueling.

command, control, communication, and intelligence (C^3I)—The "nerves" of military operations, that is, information processing systems used to detect, assess, and respond to actual and potential military and political crisis situations or conflicts. C^3I includes systems which manage materiel and manpower during crises or conflicts, as well as in peacetime.

confidence-building measures—Measures taken to demonstrate a nation's lack of belligerent or hostile intent, as distinguished from measures which actually reduce military capabilities.

Confidence-building measures can be negotiated or unilateral. The division between confidence-building measures and arms control measures is not strict; the former may involve, for example, troop withdrawals, while the latter may aim more at securing trust than limiting weaponry.

comprehensive test ban (CTB)—A ban on all nuclear testing including underground explosions.

counterforce strategy—A strategy which targets an opponent's military forces and supporting industry.

countervalue strategy—A strategy which targets an opponent's civilian and economic centers.

crisis stability—A strategic situation in which neither side has an incentive to use nuclear weapons during a crisis.

cruise missile—A pilotless missile, propelled by an air-breathing jet engine, that flies in the atmosphere. Cruise missiles may be armed with either conventional or nuclear warheads and launched from an aircraft, a submarine or surface ship, or land-based platform.

damage limitation—The capacity to reduce damage from a nuclear attack by passive or active defenses or by striking the opponent's forces in a counterforce attack.

deterrence—Dissuasion of a potential adversary from initiating an attack or conflict, often by the threat of unacceptable retaliatory damage. Nuclear deterrence is usually contrasted with the concept of nuclear defense, the strategy and forces for limiting damage, if deterrence fails. Some hold that a strategy of nuclear defense may also have a deterrent effect, if it can reduce the destructive potential of a nuclear attack.

disarmament—In U.N. usage, all measures related to the prevention, limitation, reduction, or elimination of weapons and military forces. See general and complete disarmament.

fallout—The spread of radioactive particles from clouds of debris produced by nuclear blasts. "Local fallout" falls to the Earth's surface within twenty-four hours of the blast.

first strike—An initial attack with nuclear weapons. A disarming first strike is one in which the attacker attempts to destroy all or a large portion of its adversary's strategic nuclear forces before they can be launched. A preemptive first strike is one in which a nation launches its attack first on the presumption that the adversary is about to attack.

first use—The introduction of nuclear weapons into a strategic or tactical conflict. See first strike. A no-first-use pledge by a nation obliges it not to be the first to introduce nuclear weapons in a conflict.

fission—The process of splitting atomic nuclei through bombardment of neutrons. This process yields vast quantities of energy as well as more neutrons capable of initiating further fission.

fratricide—The destruction or degradation of the accuracy and effectiveness of an attacking nuclear weapon by the nearby explosion of another attacking nuclear weapon.

fractionation—The division of missile payload into separate re-entry vehicles or warheads.

freeze—See nuclear freeze.

fusion—The process of combining atomic nuclei to form a single heavier element or nucleus and to release large amounts of energy.

general and complete disarmament (GCD)—The total abandonment of military forces and weapons (other than internal police forces) by all nations at the same time, usually foreseen as occurring through an agreed schedule of force reductions. In 1961, in the so-called McCloy-Zorin Principles, the United States and the U.S.S.R. agreed that their negotiations would have GCD as their ultimate objective.

ground-launched cruise missile (GLCM)—See cruise missile.

hard or hardened target—A target protected against the blast, heat, and radiation effects of nuclear weapons of specific yields. Hardening is usually accomplished by means of earth and reinforced concrete and is measured by the number of pounds per square inch of blast overpressure which a target can withstand.

intercontinental ballistic missile (ICBM)—A ballistic missile with a range of 4000 or more nautical miles. Conventionally, the term ICBM is used only for land-based systems, to differentiate them from submarine-launched ballistic missiles, which also have an intercontinental range.

intermediate nuclear forces (INF)—A term used to describe nuclear forces with a range of 300—3,000 miles (short range INF 300—600 miles; longer range INF 600—3,000 miles). Below the 300 mile range are battlefield forces and above it are strategic forces.

intermediate range ballistic missile (IRBM)—A ballistic missile with a range of less than 2,000 nautical miles.

kiloton—A measure of the yield of a nuclear weapon, equivalent to 1000 tons of TNT.

kinetic kill vehicle (KKV)—A weapon that destroys its target by impact.

launch-on-warning doctrine—A strategic doctrine under which a nation's bombers and land-based missiles would be launched on receipt of warning (from satellites and other early-warning systems) that an opponent had launched its missiles. This doctrine is sometimes also called "launch on positive (or confirmed) notification of attack" to distinguish between possible and actual attack. Sometimes recommended for use when there is uncertainty over the ability of fixed-site strategic weapons (e.g., ICBM's) to survive an attack, a launch-on-warning doctrine is viewed as destabilizing in a crisis situation.

limited test ban treaty (LTBT)—The 1963 treaty banning atmospheric and underwater explosions.

megaton—A measure of the yield of a nuclear weapon, equivalent of 1,000,000 tons of TNT.

missile experimental (MX)—A U.S. ICBM which is designed to replace the current ICBM force during the 1980s. This more accurate, powerful, and destructive missile could be deployed in either a single silo or mobile mode and would be capable of destroying Soviet missile silos.

multiple independently-targetable vehicle (MIRV)—A package of two or more re-entry vehicles which can be carried by a single ballistic missile and delivered on separate targets. The term MIRV is also commonly used for a missile with a MIRVed warhead or for the process of switching from single to multiple re-entry vehicles.

mutual assured destruction—A concept of reciprocal deterrence which rests on the ability of the two nuclear superpowers to inflict unacceptable damage on one another after surviving a nuclear first strike.

national technical means (NTM)—A method of verifying compliance with negotiated arms control agreements generally consistent with the recognized provisions of international law, commonly understood as surveillance by satellites and other objects in space.

neutron bomb—A tactical nuclear warhead designed to enhance radiation effects. It would be carried on artillery shells and short-range missiles, primarily for defense against a tank and heavy armored attack by the Warsaw Pact. The purported advantage is minimization of blast damage in friendly territory.

no-first-use doctrine—A no-first-use pledge by a nation obliges it not to introduce nuclear weapons first into a conflict. (See first use.)

nuclear freeze—The generic term for a variety of proposals calling for a halt to the testing, production, and deployment of all nuclear weapons and delivery systems. Proposals have been introduced in both houses of Congress, numerous local and town councils, and a variety of state legislatures.

nuclear weapon-free zone—An area in which the production and deployment of nuclear weapons is prohibited.

on-site inspection—A method of verifying compliance with an arms control agreement whereby representatives of an international or other designated organization, or of the parties to the agreement, are given direct access to view force deployments or weapon systems.

parity—A level of forces in which opposing nations possess approximately equal capabilities.

peaceful nuclear explosion (PNE)—The non-military use of nuclear detonations for such purposes as stimulating natural gas, recovering oil shale, diverting rivers, or excavating.

Pershing II—Deployment began in 1983. The Pershing II is the successor system to the Pershing IA IRBM. The Pershing II incorporates the new RADAG guidance system, making it an extremely accurate and mobile weapon.

plutonium—An element not found in nature which is created as a waste product of nuclear reactors. Plutonium can be used to make nuclear weapons.

pounds per square inch (psi)—A measure of nuclear blast overpressure or dynamic pressure used to calculate the effects of a nuclear detonation or the ability of a structure to withstand a nuclear blast.

preemptive strike—A damage-limiting attack launched in anticipation of an opponent's attack.

proliferation—The spread of weapons, usually nuclear weapons. Horizontal proliferation refers to the acquisition of nuclear weapons by states not previously possessing them. Vertical proliferation refers to increases in the nuclear arsenals of those states already possessing nuclear weapons.

re-entry vehicle—That part of a ballistic missile designed to re-enter the Earth's atmosphere in the terminal portion of its trajectory.

sea-launched cruise missile (SLCM)—See cruise missile.

second strike—A follow-up or retaliatory attack after an opponent's first strike. Second-strike capability describes the capacity to attack after suffering a first strike. The U.S. strategy of deterrence is premised on high confidence in the ability of the United States to deliver a nuclear second strike that would inflict unacceptable damage on the nation which struck first.

Standing Consultative Commission (SCC)—A joint U.S.-U.S.S.R. negotiating body, established by the ABM Treaty, which meets semi-annually to review implementation of the ABM Treaty and other strategic arms limitation agreements in force.

strategic—Relating to a nation's offensive or defensive military potential, including its geographical location and its resources and economic, political, and military strength. The term strategic is used to denote those weapons or forces capable of directly affecting another nation's war-fighting ability, as distinguished from tactical or theater weapons or forces.

Strategic Arms Limitation Talks (SALT)—Negotiations between the United States and the U.S.S.R. initiated in 1969 which seek to limit the strategic nuclear forces, both offensive and defensive, of both sides.

Strategic Arms Reduction Talks (START)—Negotiations between the U.S./U.S.S.R., formerly named SALT, which were started in June 1982 to seek reductions in the strategic arsenals of both sides. The change in name came as a result of the Reagan administration's desire to emphasize reductions rather than mere limitations in nuclear weapons.

Strategic Defense Initiative (SDI)—A proposed program, also called "Star Wars;" a defensive system against ICBM's.

submarine-launched ballistic missile (SLBM)—Any ballistic missile launched from a submarine.

tactical—Relating to battlefield operations as distinguished from theater or strategic operations. Tactical weapons or forces are those designed for combat with opposing military forces rather than for reaching the rear areas of the opponent or the opponent's homeland, which require theater or strategic weapons, respectively.

telemetry—The transmission of electronic signals by missiles to Earth. Monitoring these signals aids in evaluating a weapon's performance and provides a way of verifying weapon tests undertaken by an adversary.

theater nuclear weapon (TNW)—A nuclear weapon, usually of longer range and larger yield than a tactical nuclear weapon, which can be used in theater operations. Many strategic nuclear weapons can be used in theater operations, but not all theater nuclear weapons are designed for strategic use. The Soviet SS-20 mobile missile is generally considered a theater nuclear weapon, as are the nuclear-capable U.S. fighter/bombers deployed in the Far East and Europe and the U.S. Lance missile.

throw-weight—The maximum weight of the warheads, guidance unit, and penetration aids which can be delivered by a missile over a particular range and in a stated trajectory.

triad—U.S. strategic forces which are composed of three parts: land-based intercontinental ballistic missiles; submarine-launched ballistic missiles; and long-range bombers.

warhead—That part of a missile, torpedo, rocket, or other munition which contains either the nuclear or thermonuclear system, chemical or biological agent, or inert materials intended to inflict damage.

yield—The force of a nuclear explosion expressed as the equivalent of the energy produced by tons of TNT. See kiloton and megaton.

Sources:

"SALT II Agreement," Selected Documents No. 12A U.S. Department of State

"A Glossary of Arms Control Terms," The Arms Control Association.

SELECTED BIBLIOGRAPHY

NOTE: The amount of material available on nuclear questions and U.S.-Soviet relations is immense. This is a very selected annotated bibliography of things the committee found helpful; it is by no means comprehensive nor even exhaustive of all the material we consulted. The books and articles are categorized to facilitate use.

I. GENERAL—INTRODUCTIONS

Note: These are works specifically aimed at the concerned layperson, and intended as introductions to the material.

Freeman Dyson, *Weapons and Hope.* New York: Harper and Row, 1984. 313 pp.
Eloquent survey of the nuclear predicament by a physicist, and a highly personalized set of recommendations. Most of the book appeared in four articles in the *New Yorker* magazine.

Harvard Nuclear Study Group, *Living With Nuclear Weapons.* New York: Bantam Books, (paperback), 1983. 268 pp.
Covers historical, political, strategic and technical aspects; intended for the average layperson. Prepared by six Harvard professors with expertise in the field.

Michael P. Hamilton, *To Avoid Catastrophe: A Study in Future Nuclear Weapons Policy.* Grand Rapids: William B. Eerdmans Publication Company, 1977.

Michael Krepon, *Arms Control: Verification and Compliance.* Foreign Policy Association, Headline Series, No. 270, 1984.
Survey of subject for "non-expert" audiences.

Charles W. Kegley, Jr. and Eugene R. Wittkopf, eds., *The Nuclear Reader: Strategy, Weapons, War.* New York: St Martin's Press, 1985. 352 pp.
Intended as a college text. An exceptionally well-balanced collection of essays and articles, with a useful editors' introduction.

141

Gwyn Prins, ed., *The Nuclear Crisis Reader*, New York: Vintage Books (paperback). 251 pp.

Collection of essays by military officers, religious leaders, historians, political scientists and scientists on different political and security aspects of the nuclear issue. Based on a conference held recently at Cambridge University.

The Public Agenda Foundation, *Voter Options on Nuclear Arms Policy*. New York: Public Agenda Foundation, 1984. 91 pp.

Prepared in collaboration with the Center for Foreign Policy Development at Brown University as a "Briefing Book for the 1984 Elections." Excellent summations of the various schools of thought about nuclear questions and U.S.-Soviet relations, plus interesting polling data regarding public attitudes. Worth consulting.

Jonathan Schell, *The Fate of the Earth*, New York: Alfred A. Knopf, 1982. 244 pp.

Jonathan Schell, *The Abolition*, New York: Alfred A. Knopf, 1984. 163 pp.

Popular and graphic description of horrors of nuclear war. Schell's recommendations are interesting but not convincing as to how to get from here to there. *The Abolition* was written to respond to criticisms of prescriptions in the earlier work, and amends those recommendations.

Burns H. Weston, ed., *Toward Nuclear Disarmament and Global Security: A Search for Alternatives*. Boulder: Westview Press, 1984.

An extensive collection of essays from various points of view. Intended as a basic reader for university-level courses in peace studies and security issues.

Leon Wieseltier, *Nuclear War, Nuclear Peace*. New York: Holt Rinehart Winston (paperback), 1983. 103 pp.

Succinct, well-written, well-argued defense of deterrence. Excellent analysis and critique of various "nuclear doctrines." Well worth reading.

II. CHURCH DOCUMENTS

To Make Peace. Report of the Joint Commission on Peace, Episcopal Church. Cincinnati: Forward Movement Publications,

To Make Peace. Part Two. Report of the Joint Commission on Peace of the Episcopal Church, Cincinnati: Forward Movement Publications, 1982.

The Challenge of Peace: God's Promise and Our Response. National Conference of Catholic Bishops. *Origins,* NC Documentary Service, Vol 13: No 1, May 19, 1983.
This is the highly publicized Pastoral Letter of the American Catholic Bishops.

The French Bishops' Statement: Winning Peace, French Catholic Bishops' statement. Published in *Origins,* NC Documentary Service, Vol 13: No 26, December 1983.

Out of Justice, Peace, Joint Pastoral Letter of the German Catholic Bishops, Dublin: Irish Messenger Publications, 1983.

The Church and the Bomb: Nuclear Weapons and Christian Conscience, Report of a Working Party chaired by Bishop of Salisbury, Church of England, Hodder and Stoughton, 1982.
Report undertaken for the Board of Social Responsibility of the Church of England.

Peacemaking: The Believers' Calling, General Assembly, United Presbyterian Church, 1980.

First Report, Commission on Peace of the Episcopal Diocese of Virginia. January 4, 1984.

In Defense of Creation: The Nuclear Crisis and a Just Peace, United Methodist Council of Bishops, Nashville, Graded Press, 1985.

III. STRATEGIC/SECURITY/POLITICAL PERSPECTIVES

Graham Allison, Albert Carnesale, Joseph Nye, Jr., eds., *Hawks, Doves and Owls,* W. W. Norton, 1985.
Collection of essays discussing ways war might break out and how we might avoid such possibilities. Proposes broad agenda to reduce tensions and strengthen stability.

Barry Blechman, ed., *Preventing Nuclear War: A Realistic Approach,* Indiana University Press, 1985.

Background papers provided to the Working Group on Nuclear Risk-Reduction, co-chaired by Senators Sam Nunn and John Warner.

Barry Blechman, ed., *Rethinking the U.S. Strategic Position*, Ballinger: 1982, 308 pp.
Useful collection of essays on doctrine and arms control.

Paul Bracken, *The Command and Control of Nuclear Forces*, New Haven: Yale University Press, 1983, 264 pp.
Complete, sophisticated, authoritative—and chilling— discussion of the command and control problem.

McGeorge Bundy, "The Bishops and the Bomb," *New York Review of Books*, June 10, 1983.
Review of the Catholic Bishops' Pastoral; contains author's definition of "existential deterrence."

McGeorge Bundy, et al. "Nuclear Weapons and the Atlantic Alliance," *Foreign Affairs*, Spring 1982, pp 753-768.
Well-publicized call for no-first-use pledge. Other authors were George Kennan, Gerard Smith and Robert McNamara. See responses in Foreign Affairs, Summer 1985.

Helen Caldicott. *Missile Envy: The Arms Race and Nuclear War*, New York: Bantam Books, Rev. Ed., 1986.

Committee for National Security. *Breaking the Deadlock: A CNS Arms Control Proposal*, Washington: Committee on National Security, 1987.
Well written proposals for effective arms control covering "post Reykjavik" events.

Robert Dahl. *Controlling Nuclear Weapons: Democracy versus Guardianship*, Syracuse: Syracuse University Press, 1985.
An inquiry as to whether democratic insitutions can cope with the major problems of public policy today; by the dean of American political scientists. Argues that we need to make use of new communications technology to raise the level of public knowledge and understanding.

Department of Defense, *Soviet Military Power*, USGPO Annual report.
Published annually, contains much information. It is some-

times shaped, however, to create an impression. See review of most recent report by David Holloway in *New Republic*, June 24, 1985, pp. 33-36.

Theodore Draper, "How Not to Think About Nuclear War," *New York Review of Books*, July 15, 1982. pp 35-43.

Theodore Draper, "Nuclear Temptations," *New York Review of Books*, January 19, 1984. pp 40-50.
These two articles are sharply critical of nuclear utilization theories. See also exchange of letter with Wohstetter, *New York Review of Books*, May 31, 1984.

Lawrence Freedman, *The Evolution of Nuclear Strategy*. St. Martin's Press, 1981. 473 pp.
A very scholarly, authoritative and readable survey of the subject. Best one volume work on the subject.

Robert Gessert, "PD 59, The Better Way," and Bryan Hehir, "PD 59, New Issue in an Old Argument," *World View*, November 1980, pp. 7-12.
Debate on "countervailing" theory.

International Institute for Strategic Studies, *Strategic Survey*, London: IISS, Annual Report.

Robert Jervis, *The Illogic of American Nuclear Strategy*. Ithaca: Cornell University Press, 1984. 203 pp.
Devastating critique of countervailing and counterforce theories, and war fighting doctrine.

Spurgeon Kenney and Walter Panofsky, "MAD versus NUTS," *Foreign Affairs*, Winter 1981/82, pp. 287-304.
Excellent critique of "war fighting" theories.

Michael Krepon, *Strategic Stalemate: Nuclear Weapons and Arms Control in American Politics*. New York: St. Martin's Press. Published for Council on Foreign Relations, 1984. 191 pp.
Good, clear discussion of arms control debate, with recommendations by author.

Steven Kull, "Nuclear Nonsense," *Foreign Policy*, Spring 1985, pp. 52.
Discussion of "game-playing" with nuclear theories. Worth reading.

Michael Nacht, *The Age of Vulnerability: Threats to the Nuclear Stalemate.* Washington: Brookings Institution, 1985, 209 pp.
Thoughtful work which discusses "conditions" of the nuclear era: U.S. and Soviet national character, nuclear doctrine, technology, proliferation, and arms control.

National Academy of Sciences, *Nuclear Arms Control: Background and Issues,* Washington: National Academy Press, 1985. 378 pp.
Explanation of issues in non-technical and non-partisan manner.

New York City Bar Association. *Achieving Effective Arms Control.* Report of the Committee on International Arms Control and Security Affairs of the New York City Bar Association, 1985.
Comprehensive report, the result of a two year study co-chaired by Stanley Resor, former Secretary of the Army. Interesting recommendations, which are the result of consultations with experts. The study is professional in context and clear in presentation.

Keith Payne, *Nuclear Deterrence in U.S.-Soviet Relations,* Boulder: Westview Press, 1982.
Most complete account of nuclear war-fighting theory.

Keith Payne and Colin Gray, "Victory is Possible," *Foreign Policy,* Summer 1980. pp 14-27.

George Quester. *The Future of Deterrence,* Lexington, MA: Lexington Books, 1986.
A collection of essays from out-of-the-way sources.

Reducing the Risk of Nuclear War, Center for Strategic and International Studies, Georgetown University, March 1985.
Report of the CSIS Group on Strategy and Arms Control.

Report of the President's Commission on Strategic Forces, USGPO, April 1983. Scowcroft Commission report. The Commission issued a "Final Report" on March 21, 1984.

Gene Sharp. *Making Europe Unconquerable: The Potential of Civilian-Based Deterrence and Defense,* Cambridge: Ballinger, 1986.

Suggests "Civilian defense" as alternative to both nuclear deterrence and massive conventional arms buildup. Goes against grain of mainstream thinking and leaves many questions unanswered but case is put carefully and in non-political manner.

Gene Sharp. *National Security Through Civilian-Based Defense*, Omaha: Association for Transarmament Studies, 1985.
Outline of thesis of "civilian-based defense" by its principal proponent.

Robert Tucker, "The Nuclear Debate," *Foreign Affairs*, Fall 1984, pp 1-32.
Well written, well argued analysis of the nuclear issues. Worth reading.

Robert Tucker, *The Nuclear Debate: Deterrence and the Lapse of Faith*, New York: Homes and Meier, 1985.
Thought provoking essay which examines the growth of skepticism about the present system of nuclear deterrence.

Leon Wieseltier, "When Deterrence Fails," *Foreign Affairs*, Spring 1985, pp. 827-847.
Stimulating discussion of subject; well-written and well- reasoned. Suggests development of strategies to end war should it break out.

Ralph White, ed. *Psychology and the Prevention of Nuclear War*, New York: New York University Press, 1986.
A book of readings.

Albert Wohlstetter, "Bishops, Statesmen and Other Strategists on the Bombing of Innocents," *Commentary*, June 1983, pp 15-35.
Argument for flexibility and war fighting capability; critical of MAD and Catholic Bishops' Pastoral. See the responses "Morality and Deterrence—an Exchange," Commentary, December 1983.

Albert Wohlstetter, "Between an Unfree World and None," *Foreign Affairs*, Summer 1985, pp 962-964.

Solly Zuckerman, *Nuclear Illusion and Reality*, New York: Viking Press, 1982.

One of the best expositions of deterrence theory; critical of war fighting theories.

IV. NUCLEAR WINTER

Department of Defense, "Potential Effects of Nuclear War on the Climate," February 1985.

Finds some basis for theory of climatic changes.

Paul Erhlich, M. A. Harwell, P. Raven, C. Sagan, G. M. Woodwell, et al, "The Long Term Biological Consequences of Nuclear War," *Science*, Vol 222, No 1283, 1983.

Paul Erhlich, Carl Sagan, Donald Kennedy and Walter Orr Roberts, *The Cold and the Dark: The World after Nuclear War.* W.W. Norton, 1985.

Based on records of Conference on the Long-Term Worldwide Biological Consequences of Nuclear War held in Washington October 31-November 1, 1983.

National Academy of Science, "The Effects on the Atmosphere of a Major Nuclear Exchange," Washington: National Academy Press, 1984

Study specifically commissioned by the Academy. Finds support for the theory.

Thomas Powers, "Nuclear Winter and Nuclear Strategy," *The Atlantic Monthly*, November 1984, pp 53-64.

Thoughtful essay. Worth reading.

Stanley L. Thompson and Stephen H. Schneider. "Nuclear Winter Reappraised," *Foreign Affairs*, Summer 1986.

Major essay, carefully and professionally done, suggesting, on scientific grounds, that the global apocalyptic conclusions of the initial nuclear winter hypothesis is improbable. See also, extensive exchange of correspondense stimulated by this article contained in *Foreign Affairs*, Fall 1986.

R. P. Turco, 0. B. Toon, T. P. Ackerman, J. B. Pollack and C. Sagan, "Global Atmospheric Consequences of Nuclear War," *Science*, Vol 222, No 1283, 1983.

First public treatment of nuclear winter theory. Known as TTAPS Study after the first letters of the authors' last names.

V. STRATEGIC DEFENSE INITIATIVE

President Reagan's Speech on Defense Spending and Defensive Technology, March 23, 1983. In "Weekly Compilation of Presidential Documents," March 28, 1983, Vol 19, No 12, pp 423-466.

Original "star wars" speech.

Lt. Gen. James A. Abrahamson, "Comments on Directed Energy Missile Defense in Space." Washington: Department of Defense, May 8, 1984.

Robert M. Bowman, *Star Wars: A Defense Expert's Case Against the Strategic Defense Initiative*, Los Angeles: Jeremy Tarcher, 1986.

Strongly worded critique of SDI by an Air Force veteran of 22 years. Written in clear accessible style.

Zbigniew Brzezinski, Robert Jastrow, Max Kampelman, "Defense in Space is Not 'Star Wars'," *New York Times Magazine*, January 27, 1985.

Defense of SDI; somewhat strained and confused, but interesting because of who authors are.

McGeorge Bundy, George Kennan, Robert McNamara, Gerard Smith, "The President's Choice: Star Wars or Arms Control," *Foreign Affairs*, Winter 1984/85, pp 264-278.

Argues that proceeding with star wars will forego possibility of reaching an arms control agreement.

William E. Burrows, "Ballistic Missile Defense: The Illusion of Security," *Foreign Affairs*, Spring 1984, pp 843-856.

Pros and cons in debate.

Ashton B. Carter, *Directed Energy Missile Defense in Space*, Office of Technology Assessment, Congress of the United States, Washington: USGPO, April 1984.

Prepared under contract for the Office of Technology Assessment. Concludes that SDI prospects are so remote and doubtful that they should not serve as the basis of public expectations or national policy. Useful appendices.

Richard D. DeLauer, "Statement on the President's Strategic

Defense Initiative," Washington: Department of Defense, March 1, 1984.

Sidney Drell and Philip Farley, *The Reagan Strategic Defense Initiative: A Technical, Political and Arms Control Assessment*, Palo Alto: Stanford University Press. 1984.

Department of State, "The Strategic Defense Initiative," Special Report No 129, Bureau of Public Affairs, June 1985. "Briefing paper" on SDI.

Richard Garwin, John Pike and Yevgeny Velikov. "Space Weapons," *Bulletin of Atomic Scientists*, May 1984, special supplement.

Charles L. Glaser, "Why Even Good Defenses May be Bad," *International Security*, Fall 1984, pp 92-123.

Patricia M. Mische. *Star Wars and the State of Our Souls*, Minneapolis: Winston Press, 1985. Powerful argument for a ban on space weapons.

Paul Nitze, "On the Road to a More Stable Peace." Speech before the Philadelphia World Affairs Council, February 20, 1985. Published by Department of State, Current Policy No 657, Bureau of Public Affairs. Contains an explanation of "new strategic concept."

Keith Payne. *Strategic Defense:* "Star Wars" in Perspective, Lanham, MD: Hamilton Press, 1986. Comprehensive summary of the current debate by a proponent of SDI.

Keith Payne and Colin Gray, "Nuclear Policy and the Defensive Transition," *Foreign Affairs*, Spring 1984. pp 820-842.

Union of Concerned Scientists, *The Fallacy of Star Wars*, New York: Vintage Books, 1984.

Weapons in Space: Vol. I: *Concepts and Technologies* Vol. II: *Implications for Security, Daedalus*, Spring, 1985, Summer, 1986. Good presentation of pros and cons on subject. Contributors are authoritative and represent differing points of view.

VI. U.S.-SOVIET

Aspen Institute, *Managing East-West Conflict*, New York: Aspen Institute for Humanistic Studies, 1984. 28 pp.

Statement of Aspen Institute's International Group, a distinguished international group of political leaders, including Helmut Schmidt, Pierre Trudeau, James Callaghan, Cyrus Vance, Shirley Williams, and Saburo Okita.

Seweryn Bialer, *The Psychology of US-Soviet Relations*. Gabriel Silver Memorial Lecture, School of International and Public Affairs, Columbia University, April 14, 1983.

Excellent treatment of the relationship by a renowned authority.

Seweryn Bialer. *The Soviet Paradox: External Expansion, Internal Decline*, New York: Knopf, 1986.

Excellent survey by respected expert. The discussion of the roots of Soviet foreign policy is especially good.

Raymond L. Garthoff. *Detente and Confrontation: American-Soviet Relations from Nixon to Reagan*, Washington: Brookings Institution, 1985.

Leslie Gelb, "What We Really Know About Russia," *New York Times Magazine*, October 28, 1984.

David Holloway, *The Soviet Union and the Arms Race*. New Haven: Yale University Press, 1983. 208 pp.

Lucid, balanced, in-depth study of Soviet defense policy and attitude toward arms control by prominent and respected authority.

George F. Kennan, *The Nuclear Delusion: Soviet-American Relations in the Atomic Age*. Pantheon, 1982. 208 pp.

A collection of Kennan's essays over a 30-year period; contains much wisdom and common sense. The final and most recently written chapter is entitled, "A Christian's View of the Arms Race."

George F. Kennan, "Reflections: Two Letters," *New Yorker*, September 24, 1984.

Essay written as two letters, one to a Russian and one to an American; gives the perspective of each side. Well done.

Jeane Kirkpatrick, "Doctrine of Moral Equivalence," Address delivered before Royal Institute for International Affairs, London, April 9, 1984. Department of State, Bureau of Public Affairs, Current Policy Report No 580.

Statement of argument that U.S.S.R. and U.S. are *not* morally equivalent.

Michael Mandelbaum and Strobe Talbot. *Reagan and Gorbachev*, New York: Vintage Books, 1987.

Michael McQuire. *Military Objectives in Soviet Foreign Policy*, Washington, Brookings Institution, 1987.

Joseph Nye, Jr., ".S-Soviet Relations and Nuclear Risk Reduction," *Political Science Quarterly*, Fall 1984, pp 401-414.

Richard Pipes, "Can the Soviet Union Reform?," *Foreign Affairs*, Fall 1984, pp 47-61.

Richard Pipes, *Survival Is Not Enough*, New York: Simon and Schuster, 1984, 302 pp.

"Hard-line" views of the Soviet Union and U.S. policy.

Dimitri Simes, "The New Soviet Challenge," *Foreign Policy*, Summer 1984.

Dimitri Simes, "America's New Edge," *Foreign Policy*, Fall 1984, pp 24-43.

Strobe Talbott, *The Russians and Reagan*, New York: Vintage Books, 1984. Published for Council on Foreign Relations.

Ralph K. White, *Fearful Warriors: A Psychological Profile of US-Soviet Relations*, New York: Free Press, 1984, 368 pp.

VII. MORAL/ETHICAL PERSPECTIVES

Charles Cesaretti and Joseph Vitale, *Rumors of War: A Moral and Theological Perspective on the Arms Race*, Minneapolis, Minn: Seabury Press, 1982, 138 pp.

Designed specifically as a guide for adult study groups. Useful bibliography.

Avner Cohen and Steven Lee, eds., *Nuclear Weapons and the Fu ture of Humanity: The Fundamental Questions*, Totowa, N.J.: Rowman and Allanheld, 1985, 224 pp.

Anthology of original essays by philosophers and other social scientists; discusses moral, conceptual and general value themes.

David Duke, "Christians, Enemies and Nuclear Weapons," *The Christian Century*, November 2, 1983, pp 986-989.

Incisive, stimulating essay on subject. Recommended.

Harold P. Ford and Francis X. Winters, eds., *Ethics and Nuclear Strategy*, Maryknoll, N.Y.: Orbis Books, 1977, 246 pp.

Collection of essays by 10 authors, most of whom are involved in political/military affairs. See essay by Robert Gessert, "Deterrence and Defense of Europe," for argument for intra-war deterrence.

Alan Geyer, *The Idea of Disarmament: Rethinking the Unthinkable*. The Brethren Press, 1982, 256 pp.

Examination of the history of disarmament; the final chapter is entitled, "A Theology of Peacemaking: A cross disciplinary study showing sensitivity to theological, ethical and political issues."

Geoffrey Goodwin, ed., *Ethics and Nuclear Deterrence*, London: Croom Helm, 1982, 199 pp.

Excellent collection of eight essays written for the Council on Christian Approaches to Defense and Disarmament (CCADD), done at the request of the British Council of Churches.

Stanley Hoffmann, *Duties Beyond Borders: On the Limits and Possibilities of Ethical International Politics*, Syracuse, N.Y.: Syracuse University Press, 1981, 252 pp.

David Hollenbach, *Nuclear Ethics: A Christian Moral Argument*, Ramsey, N.J.: Paulist Press, 1983, 100 pp.

Short book, well-informed, clearly argued, both theologically and technically. A good beginning work. The author is a Jesuit priest, Professor of Moral Theology.

David Martin and Peter Mullen, eds., *Unholy Warfare: The Church and the Bomb*, Oxford: Basil Blackwell Publishers, 1984. Collection of essays by British ethicists and philosophers.

Joseph S. Nye, Jr., *Ethics and Foreign Policy*, Wye Plantation: Aspen Institute for Humanistic Studies, 1985, 26 pp.

Short, incisive essays on subject. Worth reading.

Joseph S. Nye, Jr. *Nuclear Ethics*, New York: Free Press, 1986. Stimulating, personal statement, by a political scientist and former government official. Believes deterrence can be "just," but approaches nuclear weapons with utmost restraint and sets out principles for avoiding nuclear war.

Roger L. Shinn, "A Dilemma, Seen from Several Sides," Christianity and Crisis, January 18, 1982. pp 372-376.

Balanced treatment of moral questions. This issue of Christianity and Crisis contains a series of papers presented at an international public hearing sponsored by the World Council of Churches in Amsterdam, November 23-27, 1981.

Paul Ramsey, *The Just War: Force and Political Responsibility*, New York: Charles Scribner, 1968, 554 pp.

Classic book. Argues that nuclear war can be accommodated within Christian tradition of just war. Defense counterforce warfare as over against "counter-people" warfare.

William W. Rankin, *The Nuclear Arms Race: Countdown to Disaster, A Study in Christian Ethics*, Cincinnati, Ohio: Forward Movement Publications, 1981. 128 pp.

This study was commissioned by the Arms Race Task Force of the Episcopal Urban Caucus. Discussion questions are suggested for each chapter. Author is an Episcopal priest.

Michael Walzer, *Just and Unjust Wars*, New York: Basic Books, 1977.

VIII. MISCELLANEOUS

Dietrich Bonhoeffer, *The Cost of Discipleship*, New York: Macmillan, 1959.

A classic work on Christian living.

Earl W. Foel and Richard A. Nenneman, eds. *How Peace Came to the World*, Cambridge: MIT Press, 1986.

Collection of principal responses to invitation of Christian Science Monitor to look ahead 25 years and describe how world peace had been achieved by the year 2010. Unusual and intriguing collection.

Stanley Hoffmann, *Gulliver's Troubles: Or the Setting of American Foreign Policy,* New York, McGraw Hill, 1968. 552 pp. Contains a fine analysis of the "American style" and character in chapters 4-6.

Robert Jervis, Richard Ned Lebow and Janice Gross Stein. *Psychology and Deterrence, Baltimore:* Johns Hopkins University Press, 1986.
Examination of the psychological validity of the idea of deterring war or violence. The authors review a number of historical cases, such as Falklands War and events leading up to World War II, and reach some disturbing conclusions about risk-taking, national behavior and reliance on deterrence as a strategy for conflict management.

George Orwell, *"Politics and the English Language," in The Orwell Reader,* Richard Rovere, ed., New York: Harcourt, Brace, Jovanovich, 1956.

Notes

Notes

Notes

Notes

Notes

Notes

Notes

Notes

Notes

DATE DUE

MAY 20 '91			